COMPUTER EDUCATION

Published by
Saurabh Publishing House

COMPUTER EDUCATION

R.K. Mohanty

Saurabh
Publishing House

4263/3, Ansari Road,
Darya Ganj, New Delhi-110002

Published by:

SAURABH PUBLISHING HOUSE

Distributed by:

LOTUS PRESS

4263/3, Ansari Road, Darya Ganj, New Delhi-110002

Ph: 32903912, 23280047 • E-mail: lotus_press@sify.com

Saurabh Publishing is an imprint of

Lotus Press

Computer Education

ISBN : 978-81-89005-82-5 (P/B)

Printed in India by Anand Sons, Delhi

Preface

Computer Education is defined as the knowledge and ability to use computers and technology efficiently. Computer Education can also refer to the comfort level someone has with using computer programs and other applications that are associated with computers. Another valuable component of Computer Education knows how computers work and operate. Having basic computer skills is a significant asset in the developed countries.

The level of Computer Education one must achieve to gain an advantage over others depends both on the society one is in and one's place in the social hierarchy. Prior to the development of the first computers in the 1950s, the word computer referred to a person who could count, calculate and compute. The year of 2010, a mere 50 years later from its first personal/common business use, we see the term "computer literacy" change deeply in meaning. We have on one hand the exponential speed that technology has grown and is growing and on the other hand we have the practical use of the personal computer in our everyday life. Computers are not just the boxes that took up large amounts of space with an even bigger monitor.

Taking most common points into consideration from former forms of literacy topics, the subject requires a formal breakdown of the core components. To evaluate or maintain a consistently gradual rise in practical application and social productivity from any technology we have to understand how computers benefit humanity as a whole?

The fear of some educators today, is that computer training in schools will serve only to train data-entry clerks of the next generation, low level workers of the knowledge economy. On the other hand, some hope that enhanced Computer Education will enable a new generation of cultural producers to make meanings and circulate those in the public sphere.

Computer Education is considered to be a very important skill to possess while in the first world. Employers want their workers to have basic computer skills because their company becomes ever more dependent on computers. Many companies try to use computers to help run their company faster and cheaper.

Computers are just as common as pen and paper for writing, especially among youth. There seems to be an inversely proportional relationship between Computer Education and compositional literacy among first world computer users.

As personal computers become common-place and they become more powerful, the concept of Computer Education is moving beyond basic functionality to more powerful applications under the heading of multimedia literacy. Of course, arguments about computers being common-place in the first world assume that everyone in the first world has equal access to the latest forms of technology. However, there is a pronounced digital divide that separates both physical access to technology and the ability to use that technology effectively. This book is very helpful to understand the students of professional courses by familiarizing them with the Computer and Information Technology Concept. I am highly thankful for my family, friends and colleagues for their encouragement and support throughout in preparation of the book.

—Author

Contents

Preface	*v*
1. Computer Education and Its Social Impact	**11**
Introduction	11
Learning in the Home	17
The Role of Technology	25
Early Years of Educational Software	30
ICT as Tool or Teaching Machine	49
Summary	50
2. Evaluating Educational Software	**52**
Introduction	52
Levels of Software	54
Computer as Curricular Tool	56
Evaluating Software	59
Software Evaluation Form	61
Copyright Issues	64
3. Creation and Maintenance of Educational Software	**66**
Introduction	66
Unique Medium with Unique Design Challenges	67
Design Challenges	69
Input Analysis: Communication Problems	70
Control: Many Paths	71
Displays	71
About Text	73
Highlighting	75
Connect Text with Graphics	79

Adjacency 80
Consistency versus Variety 83
Interactivity 85
Avoid Typing 85
Provide Instructions 86
On-screen Instructions 87
Teach the Interface 88
Feedback 91
User Control 93
Advertise Control Options 96
Hints for Development 98
Summary 101

4. Computers: Social Revolution in Education 102

Introduction 102
Brief History of Computing 103
The Microcomputer Revolution 106
Early Computation 107
Algorithms 109
Birth of Computer Science 110
Emergence of a Discipline 111
Shannon and Information Theory 112
Information Technology in India 113
Top Seven IT Hubs in India 118
Parallels between the Gutenberg and the Contemporary Computer Revolution 119
The Computer as 'Augmenting' Intelligence 124

5. Computer Network 129

Introduction 129
Purpose 129
Network Classification 130
Computer Network 133
Enterprise Private Network 136
Internet 137
Overlay Network 139
Network Interface Cards 140
Network Topology 142
Signal Topology 151

6. Education in Information Society and Computer Age **157**

Introduction 157

Telecommunications and Competition 159

Transforming Education 160

Integrating the Learning Structure 161

Education Monopolies 162

Virtualizing Education 163

Revolutionizing Education 164

Multimedia Enhances Education 166

Broadening Horizons 167

New Educational Opportunities Opened by Advanced ICTs 168

Towards the Creativity Enterprise 172

7. Intelligent Computer-Aided Instruction **175**

Introduction 175

The Design of MicroSEARCH 177

An Experimental Study 181

Microsearch 183

Results 186

Steps 187

Time 188

Conclusion 189

8. IT and Economic Development **191**

Introduction 191

Investigating the Productivity Paradox 192

Environmental Factors Affecting IT Investment 194

Payoffs from IT Investments 196

Challenging the Productivity Paradox 202

Policy Implications 203

9. Impact of Technology on Classroom Instruction **206**

Introduction 206

A Technology-Based Classroom Observation Tool 206

Illustrative Results: Language Arts and Mathematics at One Elementary Site 214

Model-Driven Descriptions of Instructional Change 216
Future Directions 226

10. Computer Revolution in Education: Future and Scope **228**
Introduction 228
Slide Shop 231
The Effects of Market Orientation 236
Summary 239

11. Innovation in Telecommunication and IT Regulation **241**
Introduction 241
Understanding Technical and Institutional Change 241
Incremental versus Radical Change 244
Political Economy of Telecommunication 246
Global Strategic Environment 247
Prospects for Innovations in Regulation 251
Need for Radical Regulatory Innovation 255
Achieving Consensus on Equity and Efficiency 257
Network Interconnection: A Focus for the Future 258

Index **260**

1

Computer Education and Its Social Impact

Introduction

The notion of students as knowledge workers is an interesting one, designed as it is to fit into Bill Gates's overall economic argument in his book. Many teachers would feel comfortable with Gates's definition of learning as including the finding of 'unexpected relationships between things' and it is certainly an appropriate description of much learning that is mediated by the use of communication technologies.

Schools as institutions are changing rapidly as technology alters the paradigm of schooling. We consider the changes that have gone on in how we view learning, whether this is through the views of constructivist thinkers, educationists, business economists such as Gates or the thoughts of young learners themselves.

A Young IT Professional Reflects on How He Learns?

Nic Lawrence is now an IT support professional, working across Europe for a multinational company and selling his

IT knowledge as a freelance consultant. Still only in his early twenties, he left school halfway through the sixth form when employment seemed a more attractive option than more time in education. He reflects here on his first experiences with computers, and the extent to which the IT he learnt at school has been of any relevance to him in the work he does now.

I first remember coming across a computer around 1989, in hospital for some reason or other, it was a BBC Micro. I remember it was like a cool video game on a trolley, and I hadn't a clue how to do to anything on it…so I didn't. It actually scared me.

The first computer I owned was one of those little Noddy ones, like a Sinclair Spectrum; it wasn't a Sinclair, and it wasn't as good, but you get the idea. That was when I was in the last few years of primary school. It was a case of 'Read the manual from front to cover not understand any of it and type in the example programs to see what beeps and colours it could do and stuff'. In school at that time it was all BBC Micros, and because they were still a pretty new thing to have, only the teachers loaded anything up on them. We just followed the on-screen instructions. So, up until then I didn't have any real computer knowledge to speak of.

During secondary school it was a big jump up to 286 PCs running Windows 3.x. That's when I really started to get into computers with a passion. This was not so much from learning how to add up cells in Excel from IT lessons at school, but from the 'My computer is better than your computer' argument with other students.

Back then, there were numerous computing magazines available for both the Atari and Amigas, offering not only freebie games but little operating system utilities and the like. Both computers were aimed at home gaming (remember that the traditional gaming consoles were still in their early years then): you could still get involved in how they actually worked, and learn something useful about computers in general which would actually hold you in good stead for understanding IT and computing in general in the future.

In the third or fourth year at secondary school I sold my Atari (a very emotional time I even had my photo taken with it before I sold it), and I got a little 386 PC for Christmas. That was really it for me. DOS just gave you so many possibilities to fiddle, and there was still a nice range of magazines for the novice to learn from. Originally, when I found a modem and got connected to the CompuServe Information Service (CIS), it really was just using the modem for mail, and for meeting people online after a while I had to pack that in because of the phone bills. I set up my own Bulletin Board System (BBS). The BBS really taught me a lot. There really was a whole community around BBSing, very much like regular IRC (Internet Relay Chat) users today. You found that people who started BBSs back then were split into two distinct groups, just like those that run a BOT (robot software) on IRC or write their own webpages today; the serious fanatic and the poor newbie who is destined to be ridiculed and have their work destroyed by others.

There was just so much I learnt from the BBS. How the cheapest modems were the most reliable, network security to keep the hackers out from shredding my hard drives, local networking to get diskless workstations working as a second dial-up node, user-interface design and ANSI graphics were just a few of them. The big driving force to try and learn more and more to make your BBS bigger and better was a kind of one-upmanship to get more active users on your BBS and more calls from users per day than any other BBS sysop (system operator).

Early computer software was based on a behaviourist view of learning. The programmers of that drill and practice software assumed that learning would take place if correct responses were rewarded and incorrect ones received no reward. As will be shown in the next chapter, such ideas have been very persistent in the world of educational software, and can be seen still in the Integrated Learning Systems of the 1990s.

Very few educational computing programs have been based on alternative theories of learning, although many software tools have been used within learning environments informed by these theories. A particular focus for the development of software linked to constructivist theories of learning has been the Massachusetts Institute of Technology (MIT) and in particular the work there of Seymour Papert and his research associates. Papert's development of the computer programme LOGO is a significant step in the development of educational software, for it is based on clearly held theories of learning, rather than on the simplistic assumptions regarding rote learning which underpin the work of many other programmers.

The definition of artificial intelligence can be narrow or broad. In the narrow sense, AI is concerned with extending the capacity of machines to perform functions that would be considered intelligent if performed by people. Its goal is to construct machines and, in doing so, it can be thought of as a branch of advanced engineering. But in order to construct such machines, it is usually necessary to reflect not only on the nature of machines but on the nature of the intelligent functions to be performed.

Papert continues this argument by explaining the close link between language and learning, and the way in which LOGO was designed to build on this. He reminds his readers of the links between AI on the one hand, and linguistics and psychology on the other. He also explains Piagetian understandings of learning as being at least as much concerned with the nature of the knowledge as with the learning process. 'To understand how a child learns number', Papert suggests, 'we have to study number'. The example he gives to explain this further is that of riding a bicycle. Investigating the attributes of the rider might, he explains, be interesting; but it would be irrelevant to the task of learning to ride the bicycle. That task is possible because of the laws of physical motion which govern the efficacy of bicycles; if the bicycle is incorrectly designed then no learner can ride it.

Activity in most contemporary educational situations where children come into contact with computers the computer is used to put children through their paces, to provide exercises of an appropriate level of difficulty, to provide feedback, and to dispense information. The computer programming the child. In the LOGO environment the relationship is reversed: The child, even at pre-school ages, is in control: The child programs the computer. And in teaching the computer how to think, children embark on an exploration about how they themselves think. The experience can be heady: Thinking about thinking turns the child into an epistemologist, an experience not even shared by most adults.

- ❐ Does this match your own experience of the use of LOGO in schools? If not, why not?
- ❐ Many would suggest that LOGO has been used in many classrooms in a way which is quite the reverse of that suggested by Papert; why do you think this might have happened?

Papert explains that it was his background in mathematics and psychology that led him to be interested in the use of computers to help people think, in particular the 'acquisition of spatial thinking and the ability to deal with size and quantity'. This is an appropriate explanation of the activities that many learners have undertaken with Papert's LOGO programming language. Papert had been thinking about a programming language suitable for children since the 1960s and later developed LOGO, in collaboration with others, at MIT Boston's Artificial Intelligence Laboratory.

LOGO attracted a great deal of interest around the world, especially in the 1980s when computers capable of running it become common in classrooms in much of Europe and North America. Enthusiasts seized upon the programme as offering something quite different from the drill software which was otherwise the dominant mode. And yet, twenty years later, LOGO seems much less of a force than it once was, despite its easy availability and the mentions it gets in many curricular documents, including the UK Maths Curriculum. In the end, it may have been the identification of Maths with LOGO that was the biggest problem. Papert recognises that LOGO had much to do with his background in Mathematics but he always intended it to be used in a much wider sense. In classrooms, however, LOGO has been more often used to draw geometric shapes than it has to design branching stories. In many ways the floor robots, which have maintained a presence, offer a present-day version of the LOGO experience, with the early cable-connected turtle replaced by such later devices as, in the UK, the Valiant Roamer and the Swallow Systems Pip and Pixie.

Papert continues to consider the impact of computers on learning, however, and he sees the time when schools must change, predicted by him twenty years ago, as now being imminent. Writing in 1980 about his concept of a learning society, Papert noted the obstacles that exist when we try to think of a world without schools, most of them related to the experience we have each had of such a system. Papert called then for alternatives to schools which would not be an absence of schooling but 'elaborated models of the nonschool activities in which children would engage'.

Papert has more recently addressed the issue of schooling in a book which looks at the impact that computers in the home are having on learning processes. Papert makes little mention of school or schooling but concentrates instead on the learning that takes place between and around children and computers. He contrasts what he sees as the two approaches taken by the designers of computer and video games: the instructionist and the constructionist. The instructionist the current version of the drill and practice designer he describes as 'school-style learning in the context of a game. The machine asks a question. The kid responds. The machine creates a threat in the game. The kid responds. By some sleight of language this is called interactive'. Constructionist designers, on the other hand, would prefer that the child designed the game.

It is interesting to note the use here of constructionism rather than the more usual constructivism. Constructivist learning theory, rooted in the theories of Vygotsky and much discussed over the last twenty years, has been very influential among the academic world but has yet to affect to any great extent some instruments of education such as the UK National Curriculum or general mainstream British teacherly practice.

Papert and his collaborator Idit Harel have written of constructionism as the dominant ideology associated with the Epistemology and Learning Research Group at MIT. As in his earlier writing, Papert tends to situate constructionism here as in opposition to instructionism, but he is at pains to stress that this is not to criticise the latter, but should rather serve to indicate the difference. One example he gives is from the world of mathematics teaching:

> A growing awareness of the importance of home learning is apparent in the 1991 volume, but it is more fully developed in Papert's most recent book, which deals with the technologically connected family. It is to the home that we must look in order to understand some of the far-reaching changes that have taken place in the availability to young people of alternative methods of learning.

Learning in the Home

One outcome of the 1960s and 1970s, particularly in the USA, has been an increase in the numbers of children who are educated at home, usually by parents. The home-schooling movement may have had its roots in the hippie generation and the communal lifestyle, but it has become a socially acceptable choice within some social groupings, especially for those who are relatively affluent and can therefore devote the necessary time to the task.

Much of the criticism of home-schooling has referred not to any diminution of educative possibilities where parents are the teachers but to a general concern about the lack of social interaction for the child, even in the largest of families. The Internet has come as a boon to the movement, offering as it does the possibility for interaction between the homeschooled children of all those families involved. It provides also the crucial support and approval needed by parents who have made the momentous decision to take their children out of the school system.

To those outside the cyber world of online support what we were doing was strange at best, dangerous at worst. But to the hundreds of thousands of us who chat, encourage, love, and cry with one another via the Internet it was a normal phenomenon. I was surprised how many homeschoolers I met online have gone out of their way to meet other homeschooling moms in real life.

The Home Education magazine Web site lists an extensive list of online resources to advise on everything from correspondence programmes to laws and regulations (http://www.home-ed-magazine.com/HSRSC/hsrscgn.html). The Canadian Alliance of Home Schoolers was formed in 1979 and now estimates that 30,000 families are educating their children at home in that country. Many home-schooling sites act as advertisements for their authors' books as well as meeting places for participants. This is true of Home School Zone, which also has an extensive series of links to activities in many different countries.

The UK site lists two organisations: Education Otherwise, formed in 1977, and the much newer Home Education Advisory Service, launched in 1999, presumably in response to an increased size in the market for such an offering. Both agencies sell a number of booklets and offer advice and a subscription service for parents.

The aims of Education otherwise are to:

- Encourage learning outside the school system.
- Re-affirm that parents have the primary responsibility for their children's education and that they have the right to exercise this responsibility by educating them out of school.
- Establish the primary right of children to have full consideration given to their wishes and feelings about their education.

Even in homes where children have continued to attend school in a traditional way, the effects of technology have often been noted by parents, especially where they may themselves have a developed understanding of what is taking place. This is certainly true of Linda Spear, a parent who is also a senior IT adviser in Cambridgeshire. Aware of the potential of technology, she shares her observations here of her son's growing understanding and sophisticated use of technologies unknown to previous generations. She begins by describing his easy confidence with the paramount communicative technology of his generation: the mobile phone.

My youngest son is part of a sibling group of three and one of the things I notice about their behaviour is how easily they communicate with each other using text messaging on their mobile phones. I felt excluded and wanted to join in as I watched how they switched on the text messaging option, and I sat transfixed by their dexterity in tapping in text. Soon I did it too: it was faster than e-mail, more personal and very inclusive. This technology is touching many more lives than personal computers but still some will miss out.

The really exciting discovery of tussling with a problem until he found a solution, or testing a theory, came from outside that environment. He and his friends accept that school will not provide all the challenges they need to grow intellectually. My son's thinking processes are sophisticated beyond his real level of experience. Yet he is still a young person growing up, and complicated and adolescent feelings still lead his life.

We realised early on this particular child had a talent for thinking long and hard about learning and he could generalise at a young age. His play tools were not nice tidy Lego sets which made kits but lots of mixed up pieces of Lego and other materials to imagine with. He was encouraged to 'jump the hoops' at his primary school and in return we provided him with computers and electronic gadgets that entranced and engaged him.

He thinks about scientific and mathematical ideas as if they were everyday, not because he is gifted or even talented, though as his mother I am sure he is all of these! It is because the opportunity to develop and focus on a real passion and interest was encouraged and funded by his parents. His own time was his contribution.

So how did we know that he would not waste the resources he was given? We didn't: we took the view that he would pick things up, work with them, seek help and support when he wanted it and would leave it when he needed to think about something else. He often came back to something abandoned months before.

His room is a tip. To him and his friends its a place where they construct and build and make. The computer for them is another construction kit and talking with other people who are also constructors, whether of physical things such as robots, or of ideas, is normal to him. Interestingly, each of his close friends is similar to him but has completely different talents, whether these be in art or music. None of them is awed by the other's talents; they are totally relaxed about the fact that they have something school doesn't provide: a sense of identity.

Spear's comments show not just the depth of her awareness of her son's learning and her understanding of the potential of technology to meet adolescent needs, but also her developed perception of the changes that are happening in young people's lives as a result of their appropriation of technologies that offer something to them.

Her son uses the Short Message Service (SMS) on his mobile phone not because someone sold him the idea through advertising or because he has been told to do so; he uses it because it meets his personal and very typically adolescent need for easy and private communication with his peers. Crucially, technology is for him all about true interaction; he has nothing in common with the reductive and inaccurate stereotype of the adolescent 'mouse potato', slumped passively in front of his computer screen. That stereotype has far more validity for the incomplete assumption of these technologies by older generations than it does for the young people for whom such devices have always been available.

There is an interesting example here of the role of parents in the educative process. Spear's decision to fund her son's interests is the enlightened decision of a thoughtful educationist, and has little in common with the parent who buys a computer because advertising has suggested it will be advantageous. Such decisions do not come cheap but they do hold up a pattern of education in which the school as a site for learning is just one of several contexts that are relevant. As Illich reminds us, 'We have all learned most of what we know outside school. Pupils do most of their learning without, and often despite, their teachers'.

Papert knows this too, but sees the school as an intermediate stage surrounded by learning experiences which may be more meaningful and long-lasting. He describes the young child's experience of 'home-style learning' as being 'self-directed, experiential, (and) nonverbal'. There then follows a period of 'school-style learning', where the child can no longer learn unless 'adults are willing to explain or teach'. Finally, the child escapes school-style learning, and 'the pursuit of knowledge is once more under the learner's control'.

This is a persuasive, neat and convincing model, although not one which is generally accepted. It begs many questions, not least the assumption that school is one experience rather than many: the child attending a large inner-city comprehensive has nothing like the same experience of school as her counterpart attending a private residential school. Even such unconventional establishments as Summer Hill School still carry the label 'school', but what happens in them may be nearer to Papert's home-style learning.

In his most recent book Papert gives most of his attention to what is happening in the home, a household which he suggests contains a connected family which needs to bridge what he characterises as a digital generation gap. Concerning himself with a group of young people who have been described as the N-Gen the Net Generation his basic thesis revolves around the implications of the 'love affair' he perceives between children and computers, a state of affairs he claims to have seen in many different parts of the world.

Everywhere, with very few exceptions, I see the same gleam in their eyes, the same desire to appropriate this thing. And more than wanting it, they seem to know that in a deep way it already belongs to them. They know they can master it more easily and more naturally than their parents. They know they are the computer generation.

It is precisely romanticism of this order that has tended to diminish Papert in the eyes of some of his critics. Seen as a futurologist and populist by some, he has often been unfairly criticised by those who have read only his more popular texts. *The Connected Family*, from which the quotation above is taken, is not an overly academic book but one aimed at parents, and it is the less widely known books such as *Constructionism* which contain the fully elaborated arguments appropriate for academic circles. *The Connected Family* is also an indication of the consistency of Papert's arguments; the points he makes here are only contemporary re-phrasings of those he has been making ever since the publication of *Mindstorms*. Of course, technology has moved on since *Mindstorms* and *The Connected Family* comes with an accompanying CDROM and a linked Web site.

Considering learning from a parental point of view, Papert suggests that Western shopping malls offer parents two conflicting views of learning: the quiet non-technological status-laden bookshop and the CDROM-aware technological toy or computer shop. When he looks at what is available as educational software, Papert sees too often an impoverished version of what might be possible, based on flawed or incomplete theories of learning and an increasingly rapid return to an environment dominated by rote and drills. The images may be more complex, animated or video-enhanced, but the activities are too often those which were largely rejected by educationists up to twenty years ago.

Parents, of course, are a new and much larger group to sell to, and it is clear that it is some ill-defined notion of educational value and support that persuades many parents to spend large sums of money on a computer for their children. Having spent the money, they may not notice that for much of the time it is not the CDROM encyclopaedia that is being used but a flight simulator, or that the Internet connection is used not as an online library but in order to play *Quake* and other Internet-enhanced games with young people around the world.

Papert goes on to outline to parents the oppositional modes of computer use that have concerned him for many years, although the instructionist-constructionist axis is here modified to that of behaviourism or constructivism. He does not, however, suggest that one is good and the other bad, rather that both kinds of learning are real but that there needs to be a balance between them. Educational software has always relied heavily on behaviourist understandings of learning, and so have many schools; and Papert is less than convinced that school is an appropriate site for learning, at least in its North American form.

Schools may have changed, he suggests, but only to a degree. He notes that the use of word processors has become uniform and unmarked, but suggests that it would be insupportable for anything else to be the case. Bigger change, the 'megachange' he hopes for, is quite different.

Activity, of course I do not suggest that we run out waving banners and demanding megachange tomorrow. Microchange is meant to represent the end of the scale that should be implemented now. Megachange is meant to represent an ideal that gives direction to smaller changes we can strive for right away.

- ❐ What microchanges have you seen (in relation to ICT) during your teaching career?
- ❐ Your school's ICT Development Plan could be said to be a plan for megachange—is it? If not, why are Development Plans not used in this way?

  Papert uses the privileges of age and experience to paint a picture of upswings and downswings in technology use in schools. His interpretation can be summarised as:
- ❐ Early 1960s: first great enthusiasm.
- ❐ 1970s: enthusiasm subsides—then microcomputers create bigger romantic visions.
- ❐ Early 1980s: expressive use of computers dominant in the few schools that have them.
- ❐ 1980s: use of computers becomes routine and traditional in nature.
- ❐ 1990s: next romantic period related to the Internet and cyberspace.

This is a persuasive model and certainly holds good within a British context. The first great enthusiasm arrived here a little later than in the USA, and was mostly linked to the home computing and programming possibilities of the BBC computer; but it was certainly a romantic period in the widest sense of the word. Early school uses of the microcomputer were often both expressive and essentially arts-based. Word processing quickly became a key activity, but at that time it was more likely to be seen as a creative as well as a productive tool. Desktop publishing programs, now almost totally superseded by the extensive tools in current word processors, offered a range of possibilities which related to changing the look of the text. The first programs which offered a choice of fonts for printing were very influential; although teachers of English may have felt they took pupils away from communicating meaning in words, they certainly opened up the possibilities of sharing meaning through image, colour and form.

Later in the 1980s computer use became much more routine in the UK and other developed countries and the drill and practice programs gained supremacy, an achievement which they have largely maintained. The first real threat to these reductive activities with computers has been the romantic flowering of cyberspace with all its associated misunderstandings, hopelessly overstated hype and ecstatic gurglings.

The Role of Technology

For many educationists, a key to the real potential of the computer lies in its ability to promote collaboration. This may be of the most immediate kind, with two or three children working together to compose a text, or it may be much more complex with the same young people making use of online contacts to discuss, reformulate, test models and learn from others.

The greater availability of the Internet has offered new mechanisms for these activities. Synchronous communication, in particular, has been seized upon by young people who are hungry for communication but may be challenged by coping with the concepts they want to discuss in more traditional settings. Synchronous communication on the Internet originally developed through the use of Internet Relay Chat (IRC), a Finnish invention which allows two or more people, connected to the Internet at the same time, to exchange text, graphics and sound with each other. More recently, online chat on the Web has made this facility even more widely available, and it has been suggested that this has been at least partly responsible for the rapid rise in the numbers of women and girls who are online.

A synchronous communication has a much longer history since it is technologically less demanding, although intellectually very challenging for those who use it. First available in the form of newsgroups (Usenet) and Bulletin Board Systems (BBS), asynchronous communication is now usually to be found in the Web forums which multiplied at the end of the 1990s, examples including Yahoo Clubs, Microsoft Communities, Onelist mailing lists and many others. Maintaining the line or argument in an asynchronous communication is extremely difficult; it is for this reason that so much of what is said is both bad-tempered and irritable. Contributors misunderstand or breach conventions, answer a message without noticing that this has already been done, or commit the worst breach of 'Netiquette' by sending a personal reply to a whole online community.

It is within adult asynchronous communications, however, that this degree of irritation and unskilled use is most pronounced. Among younger and more expert users there is often greater tolerance and a considerably more developed understanding of the process, which itself leads to fewer errors. Asynchronous communication has also been formalised within the educational system by the adoption of tools such as First Class, Learning Space and WebCT. All of these commercial tools aim to harness both synchronous and asynchronous communication and manage it within the traditional setting of a course at a particular institution. These tools can be used to replace a course with a distance education model, or to provide online support for a course which also involves face-to-face contact.

Unfortunately, as research has shown, learners within formal educational settings, especially those who are not technologically expert or who do not have ready access to an adequate level of resources, will not use these tools as their online instructors had hoped they would do. Much work remains to be done before educators learn how to use synchronous and asynchronous communication effectively within formal learning structures.

Illich foresaw the use of computers to create communities of learners. Writing about the need for skills exchanges, learning situations in which people learn from each other rather than playing the roles of teacher and taught, he envisages computer uses which are now totally routine.

The operation of a peer-matching network would be simple. The user would identify himself by name and address and describe the activity for which he sought a peer. A computer would send him back the names and addresses of all those who had inserted the same description. It is amazing that such a simple utility has never been used on a broad scale for publicly valued activity.

In its most rudimentary form, communication between client and computer could be established by return mail. In big cities typewriter terminals could provide instantaneous responses. The only way to retrieve a name and address from the computer would be to list an activity for which a peer was sought. People using the system would become known only to their potential peers.

A complement to the computer could be a network of bulletin boards and classified newspaper ads, listing the activities for which the computer could not produce a match. No names would have to be given. Interested readers would then introduce their names into the system. A publicly supported peer-match network might be the only way to guarantee the right of free assembly and to train people in the exercise of this most fundamental civic activity.

With computers now able to accomplish even more than Illich foresaw, it is striking to note that his vision, of a 'publicly supported peer-match network' is an apt description of some of the most popular uses of the World Wide Web. He even uses the analogy of a web when looking forward to alternatives to the present system, when he states that 'the alternative to scholastic funnels is a world made transparent by true communication webs'.

Does the Learner Need a Teacher?

No discussion of the role of the learner can avoid grappling with that of the teacher, and the extent to which teaching and learning may or may not be connected. Like learners, teachers can operate in many different models, each with their own motivations, desires and beliefs. One way of distinguishing between different teacherly styles is to consider the mental models each teacher appears to be using.

Most educational systems do not respond quickly to technological advances. Schools, colleges and universities are, by their very nature, conservators of prior knowledge, accepted understandings and proven methodologies. The teacher who has learnt using one technology is not likely to move readily to others unless clear and irrefutable evidence is provided of the efficacy of doing so.

It is easy to forget how much change has been seen in learning technologies by the current generation of teachers. By no means at the end of my career now, I am nevertheless old enough to be able to stun my current student teachers by describing my use of what we called a 'dip-in pen' at my inkwell-equipped desk at Devizes Road Primary School in Wiltshire in the 1950s and 1960s. Ballpoint pens were forbidden by many teachers then, since it was thought that they encouraged sloppy writing. Felt-tip pens had been invented just and I well remember that my infant teacher had one: a mysterious-smelling sleek black object it was too, in a velvet-lined case. It was used on special occasions only, usually to make flash cards for reading.

By my grammar school years, technology, for students at least, had moved only as far as the fountain pen: an interesting demonstration of the power of levers and pumps for physicists, but an ever-present potential for disaster in the pockets of a schoolboy. The sudden arrival of the cartridge loading pen created considerable excitement, but not as much as there would be a little later when the school was told at assembly that we were moving into the future since teaching machines would be arriving.

Technology before Computers the Short Reign of the Teaching Machine

The short and disappointing history of the teaching machine is worthy of more attention than can be given to it here. Thought of as the latest technology in the early 1960s, teaching machines were in fact no more than microfiche readers full of multiple choice questions, often related to aspects of the mathematics or physics curriculum. At Bishop Wordsworth Grammar School they were proudly installed in a science laboratory, taking up much of the space previously available for experiments, and we duly set to work with great excitement. Unfortunately, the excitement lasted for little more than a lesson or two, and the activity soon became extremely tedious. What happened to the machines was not vouchsafed to this unimportant schoolboy, but they may languish still in some far cupboard, ready to be unearthed for a museum display in the future.

We are reminded here of what has been sometimes described as the pendulum of educational innovation, which seems to swing from one extreme to the other and never stops in the middle. Attributing this paradigm to one of the professors who taught her, Mellon also notes that it is often the 'technology zealots' who start the pendulum swinging. Mellon's technology zealots may of course be Papert's teacher enthusiasts, and the differing terminology each author uses says much about their respective beliefs. Mellon, although herself a Professor in an Educational Technology department, is convinced of the centrality of the teacher, whatever other resources may be available: 'Technology cannot guarantee learning; students cannot be forced to learn; learning styles differ widely; and teachers are more important than even the most sophisticated educational tools'.

In the meantime, work continued in Californian garages and technology research departments on the future form of computing. By the 1960s, much of the development work that would lead to a desktop computer usable in the classroom was already complete. Although the first computers did not have monitors they produced their output on punch tape it had already been noted that writing could be a use for them. Rheingold describes how Douglas Engelbart proposed a kind of computerised writing device in 1963. Much of the early development of word processing was completed in order to allow programmers to reconfigure hardware and write software, rather than as the creation of a tool for end-users. However, although the ideas were there, the technology to deliver it was not.

Making computers usable was a major focus for developers, and it is the success in this area that sent the PC surging into education, at least in the classrooms of enthusiasts. Engelbart, early advocate of computers for writing, also invented the mouse pointing device when working at ARC, the Augmentation Research Centre in the USA. His influence has been considerable; it would be difficult to imagine computers today without word processing or the mouse.

Early Years of Educational Software

Much of the early work on computer interfaces was influenced by psychological perspectives. The Apple

Macintosh interface, in many ways the most influential graphical user interface (GUI), was produced in this way. It is largely because of the Apple Mac that we now use an icon-driven interface controlled by a mouse on all computer platforms.

Alan Kay in his work on human-computer interaction was much influenced by psychological perspectives. One of his mentors was Seymour Papert at MIT. Rheingold suggests that Kay was very much influenced by the theories of Jean Piaget, Jerome Bruner and other psychologists who were 'modelling the learning processes on the idea of exploration'.

The hypothesis held in common by these psychologists was that we discover the world by feeling our way around in it with all our senses, manipulating it with our hands, tracking it with our eyes and ears.

None of this emphasis on play, exploration and psychology seems to have transferred to the early computer programs produced for use in schools. For the most part, these were drill and practice Maths games, reading activities involving rote learning of words or spellings, interesting but aimless branching adventures and databases without content or purpose. But it was all very exciting at the time for those teachers who were open to new ways of working.

The state of school computer use in the UK during the 1980s can be better understood by examining the range of software in use in the Inner London Education Authority's schools. The ILEA had long noted that software was of critical importance in the appropriate use of computers in classrooms, and was to become a major developer of software itself. As early as 1974, the issue of educational software was being discussed in what was by then the ninth ILEA Computer Studies Newsletter.

Computer Software Packages in Education are upon us or will be in a short while. It is of paramount importance that we understand clearly what are these packages and what are their aims.... Where a computer software package in industry is aimed at economic efficiency and is evaluated against such an aim, a similar package in education is aimed at efficiency in learning and must be evaluated against such.

Further, the users of educational packages are generally laymen [sic] in computing matters... The objectives of Computer Software Packages in Education fall into one or more of the following categories.

- They allow a greater understanding of the topic under study than is possible with a conventional approach.
- They save time of learning compared with other methods to achieve the same results.
- They save teaching time.
- They allow individual learning.
- They improve teaching.
- They are cheaper.
- They provide motivation for the learner.

The writer of this summary of computer-assisted learning (CAL) indicates quite clearly what he believes to be the benefits of this way of working, and the list he offers contains some surprising suggestions in the light of later developments, particularly the assumption that CAL can be cheaper or can save teaching time. Neither of these claims is likely to be made today. The writer goes on to claim that his ideal educational software package would 'enhance learning, make no extra demand on the users and need minimal reorganisation of the existing practice'. It was to be many more years before even those far-sighted local education authorities such as ILEA recognised that the use of computers would change rather than simply support what happens in classrooms.

With the arrival of government funding for advisory teachers, this understanding of the irrevocable change capable of being brought about by computers was beginning to form part of the authority's practice. The ILEA set up the Inner London Educational Computing Centre (ILECC) and this became a national as well as regional focus for the development of educational software and classroom methodologies, especially for the RM 380Z, 480Z and Nimbus platforms of the day. At this time the main difference between LEAs was a decision to pursue either the BBC/ Acorn route or the RM, later Windows PC platform. ILEA chose the latter.

By the mid-1980s, secondary schools had been given a standard network with a set of applications, and primary schools were being provided with a series of packs of software. These were usually bought by schools at a heavily subsidised price and many of the titles were little used, although others became the software equivalent of best-sellers.

By the mid-1980s the RM Nimbus computer, the successor to the 380Z and 480Z and looking not dissimilar to current PCs, was beginning to be seen in many London schools. At the same time, a decision was made to issue a pack of software at a low cost to every primary school in inner London. Considerable resources were put into providing this pack, with some of the software being specially written in London, and other titles being licensed from other LEAs or developers.

Word processing had not yet developed into a one-programme arena at that stage, and the wide variety of programs used is typical of those preWindows days. Interfaces varied widely and it could be extremely difficult to learn how to print from one programme even if one knew how to do so from another.

Primary Discpack 1—ILEA (summer 1986)

RML LOGO

Write

Idelta

Explore

L—A mathemagical adventure

Maths with a Story 1

Developing Tray

Smile 2—The Next 17

The word processing programme included in the pack, for example, was Write, which had been developed by Oxfordshire LEA. It worked on a mnemonic principle in those pre-mouse days, with key-presses of the first letter of a command being the usual method of working: P to Print, S to Save and so on. This was revolutionary in its ease of use at the time; as an Advisory Teacher at the time I well remember that printing on the 380Z had included a whole initialisation routine followed by typing 'OUTFILE LST:', hardly a memorable or intuitive command.

There was no database or spreadsheet in the first Discpack, although Idelta, a branching classification tool, was included. This had considerable potential for analysing and organising information about, for example, the environment, but its use was little understood by teachers and, unlike Write, it is not well remembered. The first version of RML LOGO was included, and it will be necessary to return to this important programme below, since it is quite different in its use and in its effects than most of the other software issued in 1986. Another important programme to be discussed later, ILEA Developing Tray, was also issued in this pack.

The pack was completed by a range of adventures and two Maths titles, Maths with a Story (MWAS) 1 and a set of programs called Smile 2—The Next 17. MWAS was basically a set of numeracy games or activities, whereas Smile 2 was part of the SMILE (Secondary Maths Individualised Learning Experiment) project in London. Smile 1 and 2 had already been produced for the 480Z computer, but for some reason Smile 2—The Next 17 was the first to appear for the RM Nimbus, which explains its rather confusing title. The Smile programs were really intended for use in secondary schools, and the fact that for some years to come some pupils would arrive in secondary schools having already used this software would remain a bone of contention between the sectors.

The adventures included in the pack were typical of the genre, a breed of programme which has largely disappeared today in view of the current capabilities of moving image and sound. It is important to remember that the computers of 1986 may have looked a little like a present PC, but they displayed mostly text, they used only eight or sixteen garish colours, and pictures were infrequent and usually had jagged edges much like those seen only on Teletext systems today. The most complex adventure provided was L, which was subtitled 'A Mathemagical Adventure'. Only a minority of primary pupils found this at all accessible, but their teachers attending weekend training courses were known to sit up half the night trying to solve the mystery. Explore was rather different in that it allowed users to take part in some simple branching adventures or to devise their own.

Activity consider the range of titles issued to London primary schools in 1986.

- What types of software, currently considered important, are not included here?
- How do you think this range of titles would have affected teacher views of the learning potential of computers?

A year later, a second pack of software was made available to London schools. Extra copies of the pack of ten titles could be purchased for £48, a very low sum considering the number of programs involved. It is easy to forget that most costs associated with computers have fallen dramatically in real terms over the twenty years in which educational institutions have been purchasers.

Primary Discpack 2—ILEA (summer 1987)

Quest
Grass

Ourfacts
Developing Tray
Smile—First 31
Maths with a Story 2
Puff
Martello Tower
Revolver
Adventures in the Primary Classroom
Mallory

In many ways this was a development of the first pack rather than offering very much that was new, with the exception of the inclusion of databases for the first time. Quest, developed in Hertfordshire, was a powerful database although many teachers found it difficult to use. Ourfacts and Grass were much simpler to use, but more limited in their potential. However, the inclusion of database programs in the pack enabled other advisory teachers to set up data-gathering projects such as the National Environmental Database (NED) which were to be considerably influential.

Also included in the second Discpack were another set of SMILE Maths programs and a second set of numeracy activities in the form of Maths with a Story (MWAS) 2. An updated version of Developing Tray was provided, as well as two new adventures: Puff, which used more pictures than had previously been the case, and Martello Tower, set in World War II and too difficult for most teachers, although not always for their students. Another kind of adventure appeared in the form of Mallory, a crime deduction programme which attempted to persuade pupils to think about events within a murder scenario, rather like a computer version of the Cluedo board game. The last title, Revolver, was rather different in that it enabled schools to prepare scrolling screen displays which would look rather like the TV-based Teletext or Ceefax which were by then becoming well-known. This capability was seized on by a few schools, but the notion of using computers to publish information, albeit locally only, was an interesting development at this stage in the life of educational computing. It would be almost ten years before this activity could really take off with the arrival of the World Wide Web.

Discpacks 3 and 4 appeared almost together in autumn 1988, completing this extensive range of titles issued to all primary schools in London over a period of little more than two years. Special needs had been considered by this time, and primary school demands for a suitable spreadsheet needed to be answered.

Primary Discpack 3—ILEA (autumn 1988)

RM LOGO 2

Paintspa

Point

Paintpot

Slide-it

Move-it

Collage

Picturecraft

Number Games

Write

Allwrite

Ted

Front Page Extra

Muddles

Compose

Primary Discpack 4—ILEA (autumn 1988)

Key

Grasshopper

Drawmouse

Art & Time

News Bulletin

Maths Investigations

SlimWam 2
Teaching with a Micro 1-5
Random Arrivals
All Done By Numbers
Hazard and Rescue
Archipelago
Voyage to the Stars

In many ways, these two Discpacks continued the line of development set by the first two. A new version of LOGO was included, as were developments of Developing Tray in the form of All Done By Numbers and Random Arrivals. The latter two programs were part of a projected suite of variations but were never to achieve the success or penetration of the parent programme; the other versions specified by the original author, Bob Moy, were never developed by the ILEA. Maths activities continued to be well represented in the form of SlimWam 2, Teaching with a Micro, Number Games and Maths Investigations. Databases were further developed with the addition of Key, for which large numbers of datasets had become available. In many ways, the addition of Key marked the beginning of concerns regarding access to content, concerns which would become pre-eminent ten years later as the Internet became, in effect, the database to which most pupils would turn.

For the first time, a spreadsheet was included in the pack. Grasshopper had nothing like the potential of later spreadsheets such as Excel, but its addition marked a significant moment in the development of a generic tool base at the primary stage. There were fewer adventures in these packs, although the two that were included, Archipelago and Voyage to the Stars, were produced by one of the advisory teachers working in London at the time. Hazard & Rescue provided an adventure creation programme which was easy to use, adaptable and which seized the interest of many English teachers who saw its possibilities.

Word processing continued to be dominated by Oxfordshire's Write, but also included was TED, a programme developed in Leicestershire LEA and including an onscreen dictionary although not yet a full-scale spellchecker. Also developed in London and included was Allwrite, the first multilingual word processing package, which allowed pupils to use computers to write in Bengali, Gujarati, Punjabi and many other languages. This programme would later win an award from the British Design Council and was widely used until the constraints of the National Curriculum and other government initiatives made it ever more difficult for heritage languages to maintain their place in the classroom.

Compose was a first attempt at using the computer to create music, or in this case more correctly to assemble patterns of sound in sequences. It delighted some teachers but enraged music purists who were offended by its limitations. A further Teletext package was offered in the form of News Bulletin. The special needs programs from Birmingham LEA Point, Slideit, Move-it and Collage released considerable reserves of creativity in the teachers in special and primary schools who were to devise uses for these over the next few years. Muddles provided some language activities and word games, and the packs were completed by a wide range of graphics programs. These ranged from Paintpot at the simplest end to the much more complex Drawmouse for textile and pattern design and Art & Time, which could be used for simple and very short animations. Perhaps the most widely used painting programme was Paintspa, while the most complicated was Picturecraft, a combination of graphics and maths.

The four ILEA Discpacks put a wide range of software into London's schools in the mid-1980s, but it is important to recognise what they did not contain. For the most part, drill and practice software was avoided in favour of titles which were at least capable of being used in creative or expressive ways. This was extremely far-sighted, especially at a time when drill programs were very widely available. Later writing on the evaluation of software has valued concentration on use rather than the attributes of a programme when evaluating it, and on these grounds many of those early ILEA choices would score highly, as they would using the 'perspectives interactives paradigm' outlined in the same paper and arguing for the involvement of teachers and students with software designers.

This involvement of users had always been crucial within the ILEA and would be taken further in the case of a few programs where the ILEA was to influence the next stage in the educational use of computers.

The Exceptions—LOGO, Allwrite, Developing Tray and Collaboration

The development of LOGO by Seymour Papert has already been discussed and it is not surprising that the programme formed part of the range of titles offered to London primary schools. It is Developing Tray, however, which indicates the ways in which ILEA was able to build on the expertise of its teachers. Bob Moy, teaching at Crown Woods School in south-east London, developed the ideas behind Developing Tray, and the ILEA took these up and enabled the programme in its various versions to be written as a collaboration between ILECC and the English Centre in London. The result was a programme which was in use by 1985 in classrooms as varied as those for infants and for sixth formers. Reading the descriptions now of how Devtray was intended to be used, one cannot help but be struck by how things have changed in British education, now that we are increasingly being told the right way to do things. In 1985, by contrast, the devisers of Devtray were far from certain that there was one right way.

This doesn't mean, of course, that there's one 'proper' way to run a Devtray session. Nothing in education is really like that. We've seen enough in the last four years from watching different teachers experiment with the programme in their different ways to know that this could never be true. As with all powerful tools, powerful users can make quite radically different uses of it and find it serves them faithfully in all their ventures. But they do need to reflect on what is happening and to be able to 'see through' what they've started.

Developed through action research and refined through teacher input, Devtray is a much-remembered programme and indeed is still used in some classrooms today. It was designed to 'tap into some of the more central and powerful processes of language exchange that reading seemed to us to involve'. Devtray therefore came out of teacher activity and understanding of the teaching of reading, particularly based on the psycholinguistic explanations of Frank Smith and others, as has been explained, rather than being the outcome of a programmer's assumption of what teaching with a computer might look like.

Allwrite, too, was an outcome of the collaborative approach taken by LEAs such as the ILEA at this time. Teachers and students had shown the importance of making use of heritage languages in the classroom, and of the importance of bilingual texts. It was not surprising, then, that it was the ILEA who produced this innovative multilingual word-processing programme, much used in the late 1980s by students, teachers, advisory services and even parents. It was developed as a result of close collaboration between community language experts, teachers and programmers, and was to win a British Design Award the first to be given to an educational software product in 1991.

One of those most involved with Allwrite at the time was Diana Forster, publications manager at ILECC. She reflects here on the processes that led to its production, and its lasting achievements.

Allwrite also gave children from the ethnic minorities a different way of expressing themselves in their own languages in the writing of stories and reports. They made signs that were displayed with their English equivalents around the school, which was one very important way in which the status of the language was raised. Printed letters were sent to ethnic minority parents in their own language which must have been a welcome development to those with a poor command of English.

There are many reasons for a decline in the use of multilingual word-processing in schools. All the current emphasis on literacy is for literacy in English. And from some of the reports that I have heard about how word-processing is being used in schools generally, teachers have not understood its potential in helping children to write, so they will not have appreciated how creatively a programme such as Allwrite could be used. (I still hear about teachers who allow children who have produced a good piece of writing to type it into the word processor and print it out as some sort of reward.) Lastly, I don't think that a Windows version of Allwrite was ever produced, and using a DOS programme on a Windows machine these days will be beyond the capabilities of most primary school teachers, if it is possible at all.

Teacher collaboration in the production of software was a key facet of the ILEA's work, and of many other British LEAs at the time. By the mid-1990s, however, software production was increasingly in other hands. Diana Forster is now working in a senior position in multimedia publishing; like most of those who once worked within IT support in a local education authority, she is now employed in the commercial sector. LEAs do not, for the most part, operate as significant resource developers in the current UK market.

Drill and Practice Returns—The ILS Phenomenon

A delegation visited the USA to consider the uses of computers in schools there. A number of issues were noted in the report of that visit, and some of these issues were further developed in two following publications. Following the US visit, an evaluation programme was set up to consider the potential of Integrated Learning Systems (ILSs) in the UK context.

It was decided that two main products would be involved in the evaluation: a well-established American ILS called Success Maker and a much more recent British product, Global Learning. The evaluation eventually lasted for three years and other products were considered in the later stages. The ILS evaluation is important as much for the fact that it happened as for what it may or may not have shown about the products concerned. No UK government had previously arranged such an evaluation of an educational software product, and the initial stages of the process were marked by considerable concern amongst the UK educational software publishers. Their concerns were linked to the decline in US school software purchases at the end of the 1980s when ILS was at its zenith there.

ILS began in the USA in the 1970s and the term can cover a wide variety of products and systems. In most cases, an ILS is characterised by a wide variety of content in the form of exercises and activities, linked to a complex management system which tracks and records learner activity, success, perseverance and time spent on the system. By its very nature, an ILS has to be an individual learning activity, and it thus runs counter to the more European tradition of collaborative and provisional use of computers. The classic ILS is much more concerned with certainties and correct answers than it is with provisionalities and discursive learning.

In most cases, ILSs are targeted at those for whom literacy and numeracy have become a problem. They are seen as remediation tools rather than initial learning experiences, and the content they offer is in most cases a rather more sophisticated and graphically diverse version of the drill and practice activities of the 1970s. This is hardly surprising given the necessity for learner responses to be capable of automatic correction; computers allow little room for uncertainties and provisional drafts. Most of the systems developed in the USA work on an essentially behaviourist model, with an assumption that a high success rate of 75 per cent correct or better is needed in order to maintain interest and motivation. If the success rate falls below this pre-set level, then more accessible tasks are presented. This may be appropriate in a US context but seems less so in the European one, where collaboration may be more sought after than competition. In any case, the success rate of particular systems is kept confidential by the developers, making it difficult for teachers to come to an effective decision about applicability for their own students.

In the majority of ILS-using schools it is assumed that learners will access the system for a set period each day, usually of around forty minutes. If all learners in a year group, or more usually all learners assessed as below a particular standardised level, are to do so, then a finite number of multimedia computers will be required. These computers must be equipped with sound cards, CDROM drives and headphones, and will need to be upgraded regularly. Investing in ILS is a hardware as well as a software decision, and it is hardly surprising that the British distributor for Success Maker is RM, the most successful supplier of hardware to the UK educational system.

The claims made by the producers of Integrated Learning Systems renamed by some developers as Individualised Learning Systems are considerable. The US advertising tends to have a greater air of certainty than advertising elsewhere, although this may be a reflection of different legal frameworks regarding such publicity.

Success Maker was developed by the Computer Curriculum Corporation (CCC), who are a major multimedia publisher. In the way of publishing companies in the last few years, they are in turn owned by a series of interlocking multinational publishing companies who in fact also own some of the competing ILS products. Success Maker is advertised in the USA as being a foundation in 'the basics'. The advertising literature refers to the acquisition of key concepts, problem-solving strategies and continuous progress assessment. More recently, a course within Success Maker called Choosing Success has been targeted particularly at students at risk. This student group is not defined in the literature, but most of the illustrations are of ethnic minority group members.

The numbers are staggering and the problem is growing. More than three million students are at risk of dropping out of school, with devastating consequences to themselves and society alike. Confronted with personal or societal conflicts, most of these students want to succeed in school and in life but sometimes they just don't have the skills to do so.

This is educational software as rather more than computer-assisted learning; the model here is of the system as an agent for social re-engineering. It is a claim which will engender considerable scepticism, at least in some national markets. At around the same time Success Maker was being advertised in the US educational computing press with the slogan 'Imagine if our kids' test scores were as high as their 'Nintendo scores'. The small print in the advertisement refuted claims that Success Maker is about 'drilling and killing' and went on to describe the system as 'educational insurance', a powerful model to sell to educational administrators, especially in a litigious society such as the USA. The advertisement ends on an upbeat note which seems to take the reader far away from the reality of the repetitive and uninteresting activities which many have found in ILS.

So we will do more than promise your students will achieve the results in the predicted time. We guarantee it. Kids already have the technology to challenge their reflexes. Isn't it about time they had the technology to challenge their minds? EXPECT GREAT THINGS.

Some research has been quite positive about the use of ILS, but in this case the course described was a specialised one taken at university level. The course was set-up with considerable grant funding from the manufacturers, a process which has occurred in other ILS projects and research. Fischer also makes many assumptions that may not be fully justified by the research, including the assertion that 'ILS will clearly pay a major role in the classrooms of the twenty-first century'.

Success Maker is distributed internationally in Canada, New Zealand and Australia, as well as in the UK. The advertising in the UK is very different from that in Success Maker's home country. As in the US advertising, quotations from teachers were included. The tone was very different, however, even though the product being sold was exactly the same.

Success Maker is built on a 25-year research and development in the classroom [sic]. It provides a private environment, individualised courses and a system of constant feedback on progress and rewards for success.

Its twenty-five year development programme has given Success Maker unparalleled diagnostic and instructional routines providing individualised courses of study for each student. The outcomes of Success Maker are real learning gains for the individual with sophisticated tracking of student progress and forecasting of future development.

The UK pilot evaluation of ILS was managed by the National Council for Educational Technology and took place from January to July 1994. The report of that evaluation contains a useful definition of an ILS.

An integrated learning system (ILS) is a computer-based system that manages the delivery of curriculum material to students so that they are presented with individual programmes of work. The materials are often computer-based, but not exclusively so. The system provides feedback to students as they work and detailed records for both students and tutor. Systems contain diagnostic elements that facilitate individual learning programmes. They usually have an on-line management system that enables a number of students to work on the system at the same time, at different levels, to receive immediate feedback on progress and, when needed, provide students with appropriate tutorial and practice sessions.

The first year's evaluation, adopting a familiar researcher strategy, indicated the inconclusiveness of its findings and the need for further research. The evaluation eventually ran for three years, although different products were considered by various teams of researchers and the whole process has itself been the subject of further research. Throughout the process, the aim was to evaluate ILS generally, not individual products, but it proved very difficult to separate these two things. The final report of the evaluation was written by a researcher from one university and drew upon the work of colleagues from the nine UK institutions which had by then been involved. The report begins with a statement from BECTa, indicating caution as a suitable approach to ILS. This was in marked contrast to the upbeat pronouncements made, particularly by politicians, at the beginning of the evaluation. By 1998, however, both the government and the targets for ICT had changed, and the new Labour government had other agendas for computer use. The conclusions of the final evaluation are measured and cautious.

- There is considerable evidence that pupils do learn from integrated learning systems. The main issue is not if pupils learn but what and how they learn.
- The use of ILS has a marked and positive effect on pupils' attitudes, motivation and behaviour. As yet evidence is inconclusive as to whether these positive impacts generalise beyond experience with ILS to influence more general attitudes towards schooling or school subjects.
- Where the use of ILS at least matches what can be achieved with conventional teaching, it offers a stimulating means of extending the range of learning opportunities open to pupils. However, the results suggest that exclusive reliance on ILS for

preparation for Key Stage Three tests and GCSE exams may have a negative impact, and imply that non-ILS teaching is pedagogically necessary during the period of immediate preparation for these examinations.

- Although teachers and head teachers were generally positive in their attitudes towards ILS and its educational impact, there are issues to address concerning the apparent gap between the acquisition and evaluation of core skills and the wider knowledge and skills tested in the examination performance.
- There was evidence from all three phases of evaluation that ILS can help to enhance teachers' confidence in IT and contribute to the development of their knowledge and skills in the management and use of educational technology.

Wood further examines the evaluation process from the perspective of those researchers who were involved in it. This overview and critique of the UK ILS evaluation suggests that the conclusions above obscure very different findings in each year. The paper argues for a new understanding of the need for appropriate research contexts in this area, rather than a situation where 'variability should, seemingly, be the norm'. The slight and arguable evidence of learning achievement from ILS nevertheless attracted a great deal of attention from policy makers and politicians. One cannot help but compare this with the slow progress towards individual ownership of computers, despite the clear evidence of the value of palmtops for pupils or notebook computers for teachers.

Activity

Consider the definition of an ILS given in this first UK evaluation document. ILS went on to attract a considerable amount of interest. The popular press and politicians were very much attracted to it. Why do you think this might be?

More surprisingly to some observers, most of the teachers in schools that piloted ILS in the UK also became firm advocates of it. How would you explain this?

ICT as Tool or Teaching Machine

The argument about the comparative values of the teaching of IT as a discrete subject or its use across the curriculum is a long-lasting discussion which shows no sign of coming to resolution. It is linked to the similarly unresolved issue of computer labs or computers in classrooms. Bill Gates is certainly not an advocate of the former, describing computer labs as an arrangement leading to little PC use, and arguing instead for a rapid move to integrating the PC throughout the curriculum with all of those PCs presumably running Microsoft Windows.

It is interesting to note that Gates chooses to feature a school from the UK to demonstrate his ideas, for it is the UK that has been the leader among those nations seeking to use ICT across the curriculum. He writes too of Israel and Costa Rica, but he could also have mentioned Denmark or Hungary, but innovation in those countries is much less often celebrated than innovation in the G7 nations and other groupings, due to their comparative anonymity on the world scene.

Individual access a computer for every student started in Australia at the beginning of the 1990s when one school in Melbourne was extremely influential. Later state-wide projects in areas such as Victoria kept the influence of Australia strong in this area of development.

This was written to describe the situation in the USA. Does it also hold good in your own. One wonders for what the students needed the pens when using their computers. Training companies whose task is to pass on information and procedures rather than to educate have often been quicker to embrace technology than have more traditional educational institutions. As has often been pointed out, there are some aspects of training that online delivery can support both efficiently and effectively:

An online catalog of courses and an online registration system take the pain out of class registration. People can view course descriptions and the dates and times the courses are offered; find out whether a class is full and how long the waiting list is; and ask to be notified by e-mail when particular classes they're interested in will be offered. When people register online, they can add a class to their electronic schedules with the click of a button. When the course is over, each participant can be sent an electronic survey to evaluate the course's effectiveness. Freed of managing most of the logistics, trainers and administrators can concentrate on course content.

But how much of this can be modelled within the school environment? It would be the Internet that began to offer some possible answers to that question by the late 1990s, and it is to the Internet and the hype which sometimes surrounds the use of computers.

Summary

- Most educational systems respond slowly and with some scepticism to new technologies.
- Much of the early use of computers in school was based on behaviourist thinking and involved for the most part drill and practice programs.
- In the UK, the local education authorities were crucial in supporting and guiding the use of computers in classrooms, especially in the years before local management of schools diluted their influence.
- Programs such as LOGO and Developing Tray, the exceptions among a sea of drill activities, have tended to survive while less powerful programs have not.

- Integrated Learning Systems have attracted a great deal of interest, but this attention is related to political aims and popular notions of literacy and numeracy, rather than to ideas about the effective use of ICT.
- As ICT has become more pervasive in all aspects of Western society, business leaders have begun to seek to influence educational systems.

❑❑❑

2

Evaluating Educational Software

Introduction

The computer changes this by making us more able to reach children with different learning and cognitive styles Ms. Ackerman is a fifth-grade teacher at a private elementary school. Her school has limited funds and after years of talking about getting into educational computing, a machine has finally been purchased for her classroom by the Parent-Teacher Association. She has a very limited software budget and cannot afford to make any mistakes about what she buys for her class.

Ms. Ackerman has the advantage of having used a computer at home for several years mainly as a word processor. She understands the basics of computing, but this is the first time she has been able to use a machine in conjunction with her teaching.

All of a sudden she is faced with a set of decisions about what type of software to use with her students. The question is more difficult than she though it would be. Does she want to use the computer to enhance what she is already teaching? Is the machines best used for programmed or managed instruction to help students who need tutoring or supplemental work? Should she use it primarily as a presentation system an electronic overhead that she can integrate into whole class instruction? Should she use it to connect her students to the outside world through telecommunications and the Internet? Should she use it as an electronic reference source with a CD-ROM encyclopedia or atlas? Should she use it as a management tool to keep track of grades and other types of classroom and student records? Can she do more than one of these things with a single machine?

Most of Ms. Ackerman's questions focus around issues related to software. Selecting software that is appropriate for your students is a difficult and challenging task. Every educational software package has a set of curricular assumptions underlying it. How do the assumptions and strategies of a particular programme fit into your personal model of teaching? In what ways does a particular model of software have the potential to change the way you teach?

One of the authors, for example, has recently begun to use an electronic presentation system with his lectures at the university. For each of his 75-minute lectures, he had put together 30 or 40 electronic slides, or "overheads." The machine that he used to present his slides on was old and took 5 or 10 seconds to move from one slide to another. He soon found that this interfered with the natural rhythm of his presentation, which was something he had carefully developed and honed through many years of teaching. Using the computer presentation system that made transitions almost instantaneous, while graphically very impressive, was seriously throwing off the timing of his lectures and his ability to interact with students in class.

The solution to this problem was to use electronic slides only to illustrate the major points of the lecture or to show an occasional quote or highlight. Thus, he made the software package meet his actual teaching needs.

Levels of Software

ROM: An acronym for read-only memory. This refers to information or data that can be read by the computer, but not modified or changed.

There are several different levels of software that operate in a computer. Every computer has information stored in its read-only memory (ROM). This makes it possible, when the machine is turned on, for it to respond to a basic set of commands from the operator or user. You might want to think of this as being like a wake-up call for the computer.

Floppy Disk: A mass storage device used mainly with microcomputers.

Once the computer is activated through its read-only memory, it calls up the operating system from a floppy disk or from the hard drive. The operating system is basically what runs a computer. It is the software responsible for controlling hardware resources such as memory, the central processing unit (CPU), disk space, and peripheral devices such as printers and scanners. The operating system manages the computer's activities and functions.

Central Processing Unit (CPU): The main computing and control device on a computer. It is also called a microprocessor.

Operating system software is necessary to run application software. Application software is what most people think a computer is primarily about. Application programs perform and solve specific problems. A word processor, an educational simulation, a spreadsheet, and computer games are all examples of application software.

The two most common operating systems presently used in computers are the Microsoft Disk Operating System (MS-DOS) and the Macintosh Operating System (System Software). When a computer is referred to as an IBM clone or IBM compatible, this means it is using MS-DOS as its operating system.

Application Software: Software written for a particular purpose, such as word processing.

In the mid-1980s, Microsoft introduced a programme that would emulate the visual look and feel of the Macintosh operating system.

Windows: Multitasking software that creates a graphical user interface that runs MS-DOS-based machines.

This system, called *Windows*, is a graphical user interface (GUI), that functions on top of the MS-DOS operating system. A GUI uses icons or symbols to represent operating software, utilities, and applications software. Clicking on these icons with a computer mouse, or some other type of pointing device, activates the programs they symbolize.

Graphical User Interface (GUI): Allows the computer user to run the machine by pointing to and activating a pictorial representation or icon shown on the screen.

A widely held misconception is that *Windows* is an operating system. In fact, the early versions of *Windows* were a multitask graphical user interface environment that ran on MS-DOS-based computers. Programs designed only for use with DOS could not take advantage of the Windows environment. When you purchase educational software, keep in mind that it will typically be designated for use specifically on Macintosh, DOS, or *Windows*.

This situation was further complicated by the introduction of *Windows* '95, which is a revision of the *Windows* system and is not dependent on the MS-DOS operating system. This means that what was a programme that began as an add-on to MS-DOS has become a separate operating system of its own. If all of this seems a bit confusing, then the situation is only likely to become more complicated as operating systems and interfaces continue to evolve.

Application software must be compatible with the operating system of a particular computer. Most computers have a single operating system. As a result, they can only run software designed for their operating system. This leads to a serious problem in terms of cross-computer or cross-platform compatibility. In schools, for example, teachers and students are often frustrated by the fact that software from an Apple Macintosh-based computer operating system cannot be run on a MS-DOS or *Windows* operating system.

Computer as Curricular Tool

One way of deciding about software is to consider how you are going to be using the computer. Taylor defined three potential roles of the computer in education. These include the computer as tool, tutor, and tutee.

Tool. The computer is used as a tool by students to extend their capabilities. For example, a word processor extends the ability to write, while a drawing programme extends the ability to sketch or produce drawings. Database, spreadsheet, and graphing software are all examples of the use of the computer as a tool. Tool applications and software are the most widespread and versatile use of the computer in education.

Tutor. The computer takes on many of the traditional roles and functions of the teacher. These include drill and practice, tutorial, simulation, and problem-solving software.

Tutee. The computer is the "learner" being programmed by the student to accomplish specific tasks. In the programming language *Logo*, for example, the student writes a specific set of instructions or programme to teach the computer to draw a shape such as a square or circle. Other programming languages in common use include *Basic, Cobol, Fortran, Pascal* and *HTML.*

Hypermedia: Any combination of text, sound, and motion pictures included in an interactive format on the computer.

Using the computer as a tool, tutor, or tutee requires the use of different types of software that accomplish different tasks. Although Taylor's model is a useful means of categorizing computer use in education, not all software fits neatly into each of his three categories. Hypermedia software (e.g., *HyperCard, Toolbook,* and *HyperStudio*) can be used as a tool to organize and present information, as a tutor from which to receive instruction, and as tutee for the creation of new programs.

Another way of looking at software is from the perspective of learning theory. A behaviourist model would emphasize the use of software that reinforces correct responses in the user. This is actually very close to what happens in a video or computer game, where the user is taught to respond to stimuli in a very specific way. This translates into the idea that there is only one way to play the game and to win.

In terms of educational software, this approach is most clearly represented in drill and practice software in which the objective is for the student to get the correct answer. Davidson *Math Blaster: Episode 1 — In Search of Spot,* for example, is an excellent drill and practice programme for helping students to become "automatic" in multiplication and division. Similarly, *Word Munchers* (MECC) provides practice in identifying vowel sounds in words. Each of these programs, and many others like them, provide systematic feedback and in turn reinforce selected behaviors and correct responses by students.

In contrast to a behavioural approach, software based on constructivist models provides the student with the opportunity to construct knowledge and understanding through interaction with the computer and its software. A programme like *SimCity* has students manipulate different variables in an urban environment in order to create an efficient or viable city. In this case, there is no precise solution to the problem addressed by the students. Students make decisions and receive feedback based on the decisions and plans they put into effect.

SimCity is an example of simulation software. This type of programme makes particularly good use of the unique characteristics provided by the computer as a teaching and educational tool. Simulation programs like MECC's *Oregon Trail*, Broderbund *Where in the World Is Carmen Sandiego?*, and Tom Snyder *Decisions, Decisions* series, provide students with experiences they could not otherwise have by creating a limited model of a particular situation or phenomenon. Dangerous and expensive experiments can be easily undertaken. Time can be compressed. In the *SimCity* software, for example, students can see the results of their actions projected over periods of 10, 20 and 30 years, which is something that would be impossible in real time.

Simulations are not without their problems. Theorists like Jean Baudrillard argued that by participating in a culture that is saturated with simulations (computer programs that mimic or imitate a real museum, television programs that tell us what family life should be like, and so on), we lose touch with reality. According to Baudrillard, we become increasingly engaged in a type of hyper reality, where simulations rather than the real things become our realities.

Although computer simulations are very useful, they are also limited. Walking through a virtual museum is beneficial, but obviously it is not the same as actually being in the museum. Likewise, listening to a recording of a musical performance is not the same as being at a live performance. Simulations can leave out vital information. They also reflect the point of view of their creators and almost inevitably have a particular perspective on the conditions being simulated. This can easily lead to biases or prejudices being introduced into the software, which need to be taken into consideration by the user.

Constructivism: View of learning that emphasizes the active role of students in learning and understanding.

Software based on constructivist models is by no means limited to simulations. A different type of constructivist software model is Broderbund's *Kid Pix.* On the surface, *Kid Pix* is a simple graphics programme that makes it possible for children to create pictures that can incorporate text and sound. The programme provides the user with a wide range of tools (brushes, fonts, color palettes, and sounds) that allow the child to experiment and create in a variety of ways. Because the programme is open-ended, the children decide how to make the best use of the programme and tools it provides in order to achieve their own goals.

One final example of the constructivist model is Edmark's *Thinkin' Things. Thinkin' Things* has been released as three separate collections for students. Intended for children between 4 and 8 years of age, it encourages the development of deductive and inductive reasoning, synthesis and analysis through a wide range of activities for students.

Evaluating Software

Software evaluation is an essential skill for teachers using computers in their classrooms. There are many factors that must be taken into account when evaluating software. Most will fall into one of the following broad categories: content, methodology, and utilization.

Content. When looking at software in terms of its content, the first thing to do is see if it meets your instructional objectives. A well-developed piece of educational software should include specific documentation about its goals and objectives.

Unfortunately, goals and objectives that are outlined in

software documentation are frequently not realized in the actual software itself. As a result, carefully reviewing a product before you purchase it for classroom use is extremely important.

When reviewing software in terms of its content, consider whether or not the concepts presented are age and developmentally appropriate, whether the software follows a logical learning sequence (e.g., does it proceed from a lower to higher level of complexity, etc.), and if the information being presented is accurate and free of bias and stereotypes?

Methodology. Once you have determined that the content of a piece of software is consistent with your curricular goals and objectives, you need to evaluate the methodology of the programme. What are the methods of instruction employed within the programme? Is it based on sound learning theory? Does it use behaviorist models, or does it involve the use of more open-ended and constructivist types of approaches? Does the curricular method underlying the software fit with the models of instruction you or your school are using elsewhere?

One of the authors recently talked to a principal, for example, who was interested in developing a curriculum for his school that would provide greater freedom and flexibility for both teachers and students. Believing that computers could help him in achieving his goals, but not very knowledgeable about software, he bought an integrated learning system that emphasizes programmed learning based on drill and instruction. Simply put, the software he had chosen completely negated the educational philosophy he was trying to put into effect. Avoiding this type of problem involves a clear understanding of curricular objectives and methods both at a classroom level and at the level of the software being used.

Utilization. Finally, evaluating software involves asking questions of utilization. Is the software user friendly? Can users stop at any time during the programme? Can they reenter where they left off? Can children use the programme without a great deal of assistance from adults (Are there picture menus? Are menus text dependent?) Is the documentation for the programme clear? Can the teacher change the parameters of the software? For example, can levels of difficulty in a game or simulation be modified, or can the spoken component in an electronic book be turned off for silent reading?

Software Evaluation Form

Check each item for the software being looked at and provide a summary evaluation.

Hardware Compatibility

- ❒ Compatible operating system
- ❒ Sufficient RAM
- ❒ Sufficient hard disk space
- ❒ Necessary peripherals such as CD-ROM drive, printer, or videodisc player.

Content

- ❒ Programme fits the educational goals and supports the curriculum.
- ❒ Goals and objectives of the software are clearly stated.
- ❒ Programme meets its stated objectives.
- ❒ Content is accurate, dealt with in sufficient depth, and free of bias and stereotypes.
- ❒ Content is at a level appropriate to students.
- ❒ There is a logical learning sequence, with a low entry and high ceiling so it can be used across a range of ages and abilities.
- ❒ Content is suitable for multiple purposes for integration into different curriculum areas and classroom situations.

Methodology

- ❒ Instructional approach is appropriate. Active discovery learning is emphasized.

- ❒ There is a high degree of student involvement.
- ❒ Students are agents of change; there is consistent cause and effect.
- ❒ Feedback is appropriate, varied, and able to be understood by students.
- ❒ Prompts and other strategies for getting the correct answer are provided.
- ❒ Students are led through the information in a logical way. Branching depends on students' responses.

Utilization

- ❒ Students control the interaction and the rate of presentation and can stop at any point in the programme.
- ❒ Teachers can change parameters, such as speed of presentation and level of difficulty, to fit the range of needs and interests of students.
- ❒ Students can use the software independently after initial help. Picture menus, simple and precise directions, and onscreen help are available.
- ❒ The software can be used in small groups or by the whole class, as well as by individuals. It encourages cooperation and interaction.
- ❒ Documentation includes objectives, lesson plans, resources, and other information for teachers, as well as clear directions for the user.
- ❒ The management or record keeping component is easy to use.

Summary Evaluation

Sources for Software: There are many ways to learn about software, both new products and tested materials. Larger school districts across the country have instructional resource libraries with extensive collections of software. In Dade County, Florida, for example, there is a hardware and software resource center for teachers at the district's central administration complex. All of the major computers and peripherals being used throughout the district are available. In addition, there is a collection of nearly all of the major educational software that is available. Teachers can review software titles and also see how different types of computer hardware work.

Another excellent way to become familiar with software is to go to your local computer store and look at products that are for sale. Many companies in U.K. like Broderbund and Edmark sell home versions of school products.

Before you purchase software, you need to preview it or get a recommendation from someone whose opinion you trust. Unfortunately, catalogue descriptions of software can be very misleading. A piece of software may look like exactly what you need, but in reality, it may not measure up to its promises.

One of the very best ways to be able to preview software is to attend one of the many regional and national educational computing conferences held around the country. At the larger conferences, software and hardware vendors will have exhibit booths where their products can be tested. In addition, they frequently have free demonstration versions of software that will allow people to try out different products at their leisure.

Most large software companies will allow software to be tried on a 30- to 60-day preview basis. If you are not sure about whether or not a piece of software will meet your needs, get a preview copy and try it. There is nothing to lose except the cost of the return postage.

Freeware: Software that is given away Free of Charge

A great deal of useful educational software is available in the public domain as freeware. Freeware is often available over the Internet, or through user groups and computer magazines. Much of it is passed informally from one person to another. Freeware frequently includes a lot of junk, but sometimes you can find just the type of programme that will serve your needs. Documentation on freeware is often limited, and there is always the problem of the transmission of computer viruses through this type of material. Just keep in mind that there are hidden costs when using "free" software.

Shareware: Software distributed for a free tryout, but users are expected to pay the developer if they decide to use the software.

Shareware is distributed in much the same way as freeware, but the developer of a programme asks the user to send a nominal fee for using the programme. In exchange for this fee, you get the right to use the programme and often are put on a list for additional information about the programme and even upgrades of the software. Shareware is particularly good because it allows you to try out a piece of software to see if you like it before you have to pay for it.

Copyright Issues

Lab Pack: Typically includes five copies of a particular piece of software and the right to load it onto five computers.

Copyright: The exclusive legal right to reproduce, publish, and sell the matter and form of some type of work.

Except for freeware and public domain software, most computer programs are copyrighted. A copyright protects the intellectual property rights of publishers and authors. Software is sold in a number of different ways. It can be purchased as a single copy, in what is called a lab pack (multiple copies for a single classroom or lab), or in a network version. Typically, when you buy a computer programme, unless there is another arrangement such as a site license, you have the right to use it on a single machine. If you have 10 students using 10 computers in a classroom, then you need to purchase a copy for each machine, or else connect the computers and get a networked version of the software.

Site License: When a software publisher agrees to make a software programme available to be copied at a single site for a set fee.

Instead of purchasing individual software programs for each machine in a school, many school districts license the right to use a piece of software. This is called a site license. Under most arrangements, a school district agrees to pay a set fee, which is usually based on the total number of computers in a district. This fee allows the district to make as many copies as it needs for use in its schools. Such agreements are an excellent way to use multiple copies of a programme at a greatly reduced rate. Publishers like such arrangements because it means their software is being used legally and they are getting a fair payment for the products they have created. When using software under a site license, keep in mind that you do not receive documentation for each site. You can often buy additional copies of documentation at a modest fee.

Some school districts elect to license all of the software from a particular publisher. Such arrangements can lead to very large savings, while making a wide range of software available at a very low cost.

In conclusion, as demonstrated with Ms. Ackerman in the case study at the beginning of this chapter, decisions about software and its use in the classroom are ultimately decisions about curriculum. Too often educators have become preoccupied with the hardware of computers and have not reflected sufficiently on what is being run on the machines.

3

Creation and Maintenance of Educational Software

Introduction

Some of what we say may seem utterly obvious and banal, yet we have often seen these "obvious" points missed by intelligent but inexperienced authors, including people who are very skilled both in teaching and in using computers, but who are new to the use of computers as an instructional medium. Diligent, committed authors will eventually come to many of the conclusions discussed here. By offering guidelines and suggestions, we hope to shorten the time required to discover what works and what doesn't. Nevertheless, there is no substitute for your own experience. We can help you reach the foothills, but you must reach the summit on your own.

What experiences have influenced our views on software? We have developed and published entire computer-based courses in chemistry and physics which have been used by thousands of students. We have carried out formal and informal evaluations of these courses. Chabay has studied motivational factors in both computer-based and human tutoring. Sherwood has used computer-based materials for learning and teaching foreign languages. We are acquainted with a large amount of good and bad educational software. We have often been asked by novice and experienced authors for critiques of their work. It is this range of experience that encourages us to attempt a synthesis of what we think we have learned so far. We ourselves, however, feel that even after twenty years of experience we are still learning about this new medium, and we hope in the future to be able to create educational software much better than anything we have produced previously.

We will first discuss in general terms how the computer medium differs from other media and enumerate design challenges unique to this medium. Second, we will present specific guidelines for solutions to some of these problems in the areas of display, interactivity, input analysis, and control. We will close with a few hints on how to make the development of materials itself an interactive process.

Unique Medium with Unique Design Challenges

The Medium

Interactive software is a new medium and needs time to mature. It took several decades for cinema to mature, moving away from simply filming stage productions to a realization and exploitation of capabilities radically different from those of the stage. In the same way, interactive software differs dramatically from all previous media, because it is a two-way, dynamic, modifiable medium, requiring active input from the user, while previous media were primarily passive and one-way. The only model we have for this new interactive medium is human conversation. This model has limited utility, since on the one hand computers are not yet capable of complex, open-ended verbal interaction, while on the other, conversations do not exploit the dynamic, modifiable visual representations which computers can easily support. As a result, there is little past experience to draw upon for guidance.

The computer medium is unique in requiring inputs from the user. Exploiting this interactive character is a major reason for using a computer in instruction. But interaction creates a set of design problems that differ significantly from those of non-interactive media. For example, although graphic designers know a great deal about how to lay out an advertisement for a magazine, they need not worry about how to make such a display dynamic or interactive. In contrast, a computer display is often constructed a little at a time in response to inputs, instead of appearing all at once as does a magazine page. Perhaps the closest analogy is offered by informational video, which often builds up displays in a dynamic manner. However, its sequence is strictly linear, and there is no opportunity for user input or control of pace or content. In contrast, a computer display not only must look attractive but must also explain, or better, imply, how he reader might interact (e.g., touch a particular portion of the screen, or choose a menu option). In fact, since the actual content of a display may depend on user inputs, the programme developer may not entirely know what will ultimately appear on a display. Such dynamic presentations, with pace and content influenced by the user, have an entirely different esthetic both from all-at-once pages in a book or magazine and from linear video or film.

In other media, physical characteristics provide context and control. For example, television programs have established lengths (30 or 60 minutes), and viewers can change channels at will. Readers can tell at a glance how far they've gotten in a book and can easily skip to a different part. The computer medium, however, does not automatically provide such information and options.

In the specific case of instruction, how does the computer medium differ from traditional materials? In some ways the computer is more limited. Flipping between pages in a book is a rapid, intuitive process, and each page has significantly higher resolution and capacity than most current computer screens. Only very recently have there emerged computer-based materials which even approximate the easy access and high-quality text and graphics of a textbook. However, the computer has some advantages over the textbook. Static texts are rarely able to represent dynamic phenomena adequately, and they certainly cannot allow readers to experiment with the effect of parameter changes on figures in the text. Perhaps more importantly, the one-way nature of the textbook severely limits its effectiveness. Lacking inputs from the student, a textbook cannot notice that several pages have flowed by without the student understanding anything at all.

The computer medium offers more precision and more dynamic representations than a blackboard. Lectures plod or race inexorably forward in a straight line at a pace which may suit only a minority of the students. Compared with lectures, computer materials are inherently self-paced and repeatable, and they offer the potential for useful non-linearity (e.g., review, additional explanation, or experimentation). In favorable cases a computer programme may be able to detect an individual student's difficulties and offer appropriate help, something rarely possible in a large lecture and too seldom available even in a small-group discussion class.

Design Challenges

Developing programs presents a series of challenging design problems. On each topic we offer suggestions on what to strive for and what to avoid. Situations do invariably arise where these guidelines conflict, and while we cannot provide general strategies for resolving such conflicts, we will at least note common dilemmas and trade-offs. Throughout the discussion, the following themes will recur with variations: displays, interactivity, input analysis, and control. They identify particularly challenging and critical aspects of interactive instructional programs.

Displays: A Visual Medium

The computer is inherently a visual medium. Because of its strong graphical capabilities, and because natural language interaction with a computer is so difficult, communication with the user will rely heavily on pictures and diagrams. Even text, in this medium, is best thought of as graphics. It is not effective to produce and lay out text for an interactive programme as one would for a book. On the other hand, the dynamic nature of the medium offers new possibilities for presenting and making use of text.

Interactivity: Intuitive, Transparent Interactions with Displays

The uniquely interactive, two-way nature of the medium has a striking impact even on seemingly non-interactive components such as static displays. Not only *can* the user interact with the programme, he or she *must* interact for anything to happen at all. How does the user know what to do? One might think it sufficient to write instructions on the screen. But sad experience proves that even experienced users, including ourselves, often do not read or attend to such instructions. A major challenge is to produce graphics and text displays that make intuitively obvious what next moves are possible. This *interactivity* is part of the unique esthetic of good computer displays.

Input Analysis: Communication Problems

While modern computers offer exciting capabilities, they do sharply constrain the breadth of interaction compared with what a human provides. Through tone of voice, facial expression, and other body language, a human teacher provides important extra information, both cognitive and affective, that a computer cannot express. In the other direction, the computer's ability to guess a student's intentions is limited.

Control: Many paths

Unlike other media, the behavior of an interactive programme is not entirely predictable, since it depends on user inputs. In extreme cases, every user of the same programme might have a different experience different paths through the material, different kinds of messages in response to inputs, different types of exercises, etc. The programme must provide sensible context and responses for any path the user may follow; conversely, users must not be allowed to follow paths that the programme is not prepared to deal with.

Using the framework described above, we now discuss major design issues related to display, interactivity, input, and control. We will close with advice on the development process itself.

Displays

There exist only the beginnings of a theory of what constitutes a good computer display, but some useful general points can be made. You want the user to pay attention to the most important things, and there is a limit on how many things the user can attend to simultaneously. This suggests keeping the display sparse and uncluttered, highlighting the most important aspects, and regularly removing from the screen those things which are of less importance and might distract the user. Since most computer screens are relatively small, with relatively low resolution compared to paper, displays can easily get crowded if one is not careful.

We offer the following suggestions for good, useful displays.

Basic Display Considerations

Let display determine structure: Make display central to programme structure. Try to tie internal data structures to the external displays. Think of the display screen as the dominant element which drives your programme and data structures. Don't think of the display aspects as a mere "user-interface" veneer grudgingly pasted over the "real" programme. In an interactive programme, the display is not the icing, but the cake; routines and data take second place to the screen.

Simpler is better: This is perhaps the most important rule of display design. It is often a good rule in any medium, but it has special force in an interactive medium where the viewer must do more than passively observe the displays go by. But what is "simpler?" It is possible to characterize some aspects in detail.

Blank space: Leave lots of blank space. Leave borders, space between paragraphs, etc. Blank space in a computer display costs nothing, yet it is a powerful tool for making the important material stand out. Use two or three sparse displays rather than one dense display to present material that need not appear all at once. It is an unfortunate fact of life that most current computers have rather small screens which can easily get quite crowded if care is not taken in designing the displays.

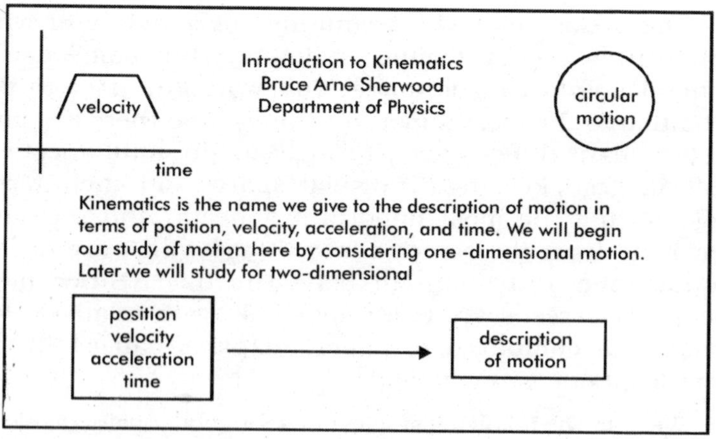

Compare the busy, crowded display above with the following display:

INTRODUCTION to KINEMATICS
Bruce Arne Sherwood
Department of Physics

Kinematics is the study of melisa:

position
velocity
acceleration
time

in this lesson we will study melisa in one two dimensions.

Information in the second display is clearer and easier to find.

About Text

Text IS Graphics

Text serves two important functions in graphical displays. First, it presents basic information, and clarifies and explains pictures and diagrams. Second, it provides general instructions for using the programme and specific instructions for performing particular tasks. Both uses are critical to the successful functioning of a programme. But recall the discussion at the beginning of this chapter: a computer is not a book. The sort of text that is appropriate to books does not work in dynamic interactive programs.

Don't use Paragraphs

When you present text, don't use book-like paragraphs but rather set-off words and phrases with plenty of white space. Even well-intentioned, diligent users have difficulty reading and retaining paragraphs of text displayed on the computer screen. Compare this paragraph with the following format: When presenting text.

- don't use paragraphs

- do set-off words and phrases
- compare with the format above

This terse, open, telegraphic presentation of the key points is particularly appropriate in an interactive medium and one in which blank space is cheap.

Mix Text and Pictures

In scientific or technical programs, authors often make the mistake of omitting explanatory text for diagrams. A picture may well be worth a thousand words, but a few well-placed words can enormously increase the impact of a picture. For example:

- Label the axes of your graphs. (Is the horizontal axis time or distance?)
- Label each curve plotted on a graph. (Which parameter value generated which curve?)
- Identify important components of diagrams. (Which angle is theta?)

Likewise, in verbal, text-oriented applications, a few pictures can vivify concepts and add interest.

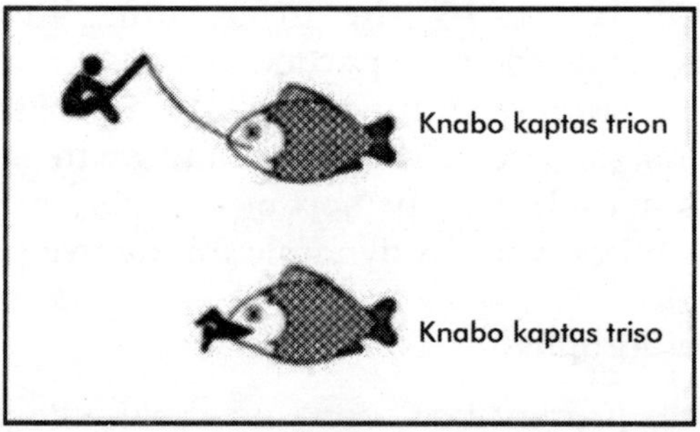

This display makes vivid the importance of the final "n" in identifying the direct object of an Esperanto verb.

Strive for Clarity

Time spent searching for clear, concise wording is time well invested. Very clear wording is essential both for subject matter and for instructions. Most teachers have had the sad experience of discovering while grading an exam that students misread a problem statement that had seemed perfectly clear to the teacher. The misunderstanding might never have been discovered, had the student not been asked to perform an action based on that text. In a textbook, by contrast, unclear or misleading wording may go undiscovered through several editions, because there is little direct evidence of the fact that students are not understanding some paragraph. The interactive computer medium, which demands inputs and responses from users, requires clear, unambiguous wording.

Highlighting

Ideally, it should be vividly clear at all times which parts of the display are most important. Various forms of highlighting can be used to emphasize what is salient.

Highlighting Provides a Focus

Use highlighting to provide a focus on the most important points. It can be achieved by the use of italics, by making something blink, by putting a box around a major item of text, by pointing at something, by using "inverse video" (e.g., white letters on a black background instead of black on white), by using distinctive colors, etc.

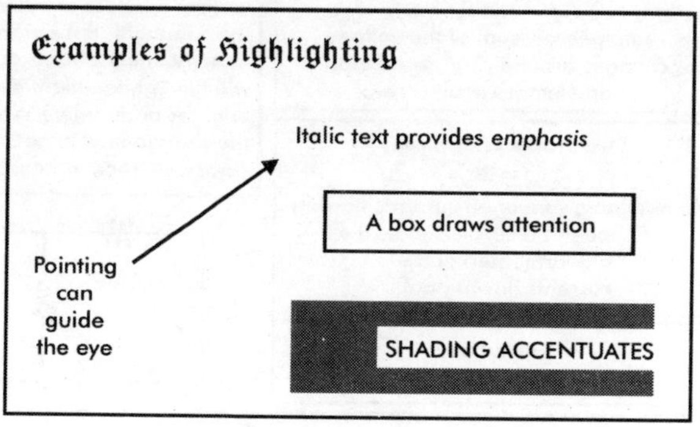

Highlighting can be dynamic and temporary. That is, once the user has done something which indicates that attention is being paid to the highlighted area, you might remove or reduce that highlighting.

Highlight Sparingly

If everything is highlighted, nothing is important, as in a student's textbook where every sentence has been marked yellow with a highlighting pen. Moreover, *using toomany colors* or too many text styles can be VERY DISTRACTING!

Make important display components BIG

If the critical element of the display is a circuit diagram, it should normally be at the center of the display and large, while peripheral matters such as lists of options or explanatory text should be relegated to the periphery or to menus which are displayed only when invoked by the user.

Compare the following examples. In the first version, the central element (the circuit) is overwhelmed by non-critical information. The user must sort through the text to find out what, in fact, is the task posed by the display. Extra text is required to refer to and identify the headlights, which are not visually distinguished as the elements of interest in the circuit.

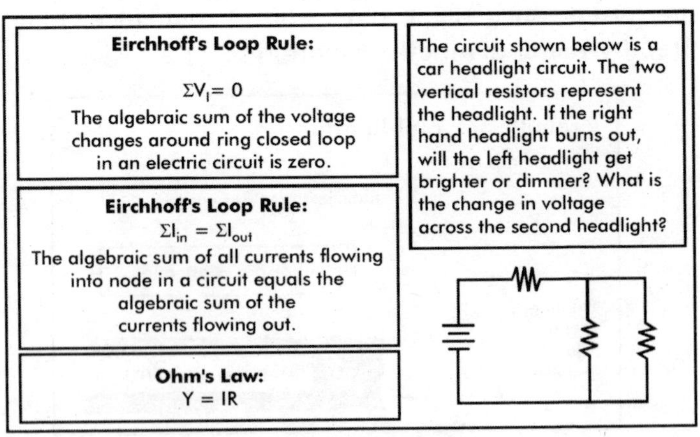

The circuit is central to the second display, with options and rules relegated to menus which the user can invoke.

Option Rules

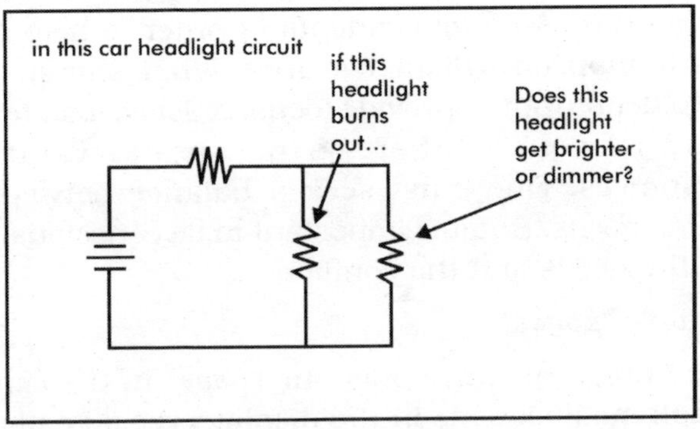

Remove unnecessary elements

Many of your displays will be dynamic rather than static: elements come and go in the course of the interaction with the user. It is important to remove text or graphics no longer needed, to make it easier for the user to pay attention to that which is still important or newly important.

Incremental Display-Building

Another way to provide emphasis and focus is by building up a display a little at a time. Here are some considerations in this regard.

Build up displays piece by piece

Do not flood the display with a great deal of information all at once. Constructing the display one element at a time, and waiting for a signal (a key press or mouse click) before adding the next element, gives the user time to identify and comprehend the components of a complex display.

Maintain visual context, but avoid clutter

Leave enough older information on the screen to provide a context for the current activity. Such context is typically more needed here than in a book because it is usually easier for a book reader to flip back and forth to review the context.

However, here is one of the conflicts to which we alluded earlier. It is necessary to retain enough of a display to maintain context for the activity. It is also necessary to remove all but essential elements in order to help the user focus attention on salient features. What should you do, remove older output to provide focus, or leave it on to provide context? Of course, there is no answer valid for all circumstances. One must seek a balance between these competing needs. But it is important to be consciously aware of both the needs and the conflict.

Use multiple "pages"

Many programs have only one "page" in the sense that only small modifications in the display ever take place, and the screen is never erased as a whole. This display strategy has the advantage of keeping a strong contextual framework visible at all times. However, one should not always slavishly follow this model. For example, your programme might detect a major misunderstanding on the part of the student which requires extended discussion. Trying to squeeze this somewhere onto the current "page" may cramp things too much. It may be much better to clear the screen entirely, display only the bare minimum of context extracted from the situation, and proceed to exploit the much larger display space now available. When you have completed this digression, go reconstruct the original display to re-establish the full context. Other uses of multi- "page" strategies include having title pages and tables of contents, or separate sections of the programme with quite different contents and formats.

Break up long texts

It is often helpful to the user to break up text into separate pieces, waiting for a keypress before adding the next item to the growing list. Building up the list a little at a time maintains emphasis (of the most recent item) while maintaining context (because the previous items are still visible).

Building up the display a little at a time is a very simple but effective technique, and one which a book cannot offer.

Connections among Display Elements

In this section we discuss the importance of connections among the various parts of a display.

Connect Text with Graphics

A general principle is to avoid describing in words that which is better shown with graphics, and this includes tying together pieces of text. It is much better to point graphically to the relevant words in a cited passage than to attempt to describe its location verbally:

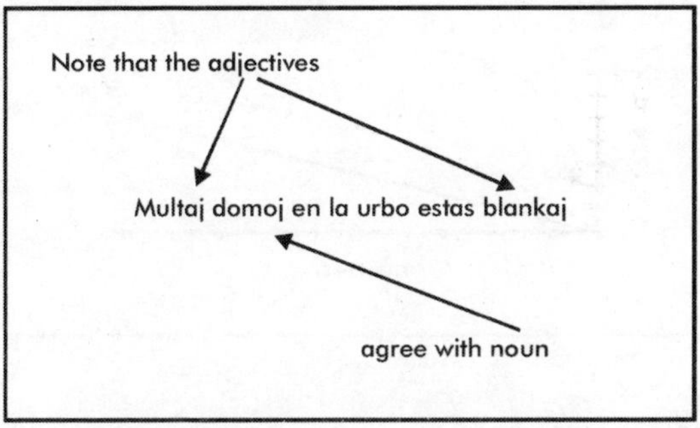

Connect graphics with text

Text and sequencing are needed to make connections among the elements of a graphical display. For example, remember to title the axes of a graph. You may know very well what the graph depicts, but you're not writing the programme just for yourself. If there are several functions displayed on the graph, consider distinguishing them with their own neighboring titles, and/or plotting them one at a time in diverse colors or textures, waiting for user acknowledgement with a keypress before displaying another in the series. As with text, this incremental approach to building the final display is an excellent mechanism for providing both emphasis and context.

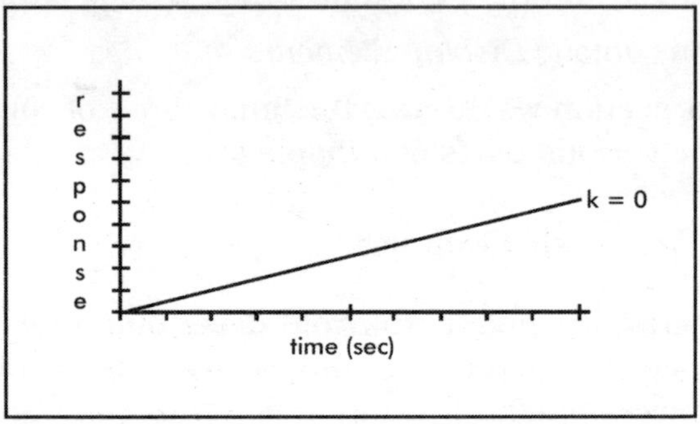

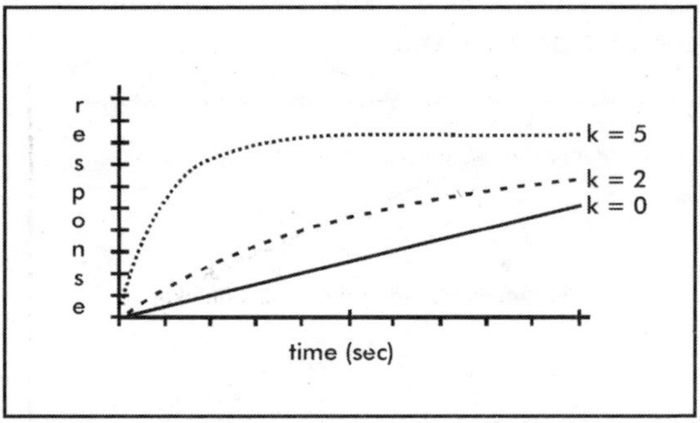

Adjacency

Generally speaking, work down and to the right as you add to a display, to provide some consistency in where to look for new information. A more general way to state this principle is that new information should be near the most recently displayed information. Adjacency on the screen is an important tool for making a complex display understandable. But when it isn't possible to use adjacency, or you need to make a link back to earlier information, use sequencing or graphic cues to make that connection.

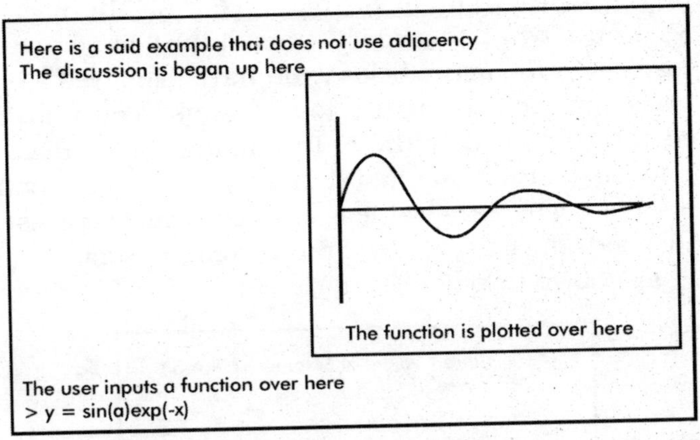

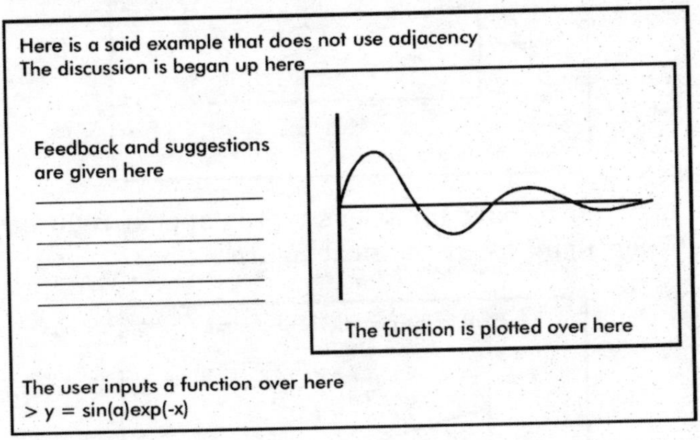

Input: Adjacency *versus* Consistency

It is desirable to establish a clear convention for input. One strategy, which is frequently appropriate, is to decide on a single, consistent screen location for input throughout the programme. Given such consistency, the user will always know where to look when input is requested. However, the requirement for consistency may conflict with other principles. For example, for the sake of consistency, you might decide that input typed by the user should always be entered at the bottom of the screen, so the user will always know what to expect when input is requested. Suppose, as in the figure below, you have displayed a list of numerical parameters at the top of the screen and have invited the user to vary them. In making the change, the user's focus of attention must drop way down to the bottom of the screen, where the value is entered. This is consistent. It is not good, since the context (the current parameter value) is lost, as shown below.

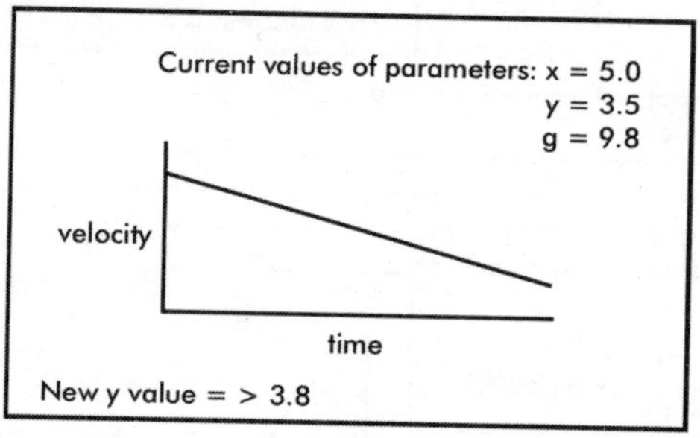

It is better to have the user's typing appear right beside the chosen item, as in the next figure.

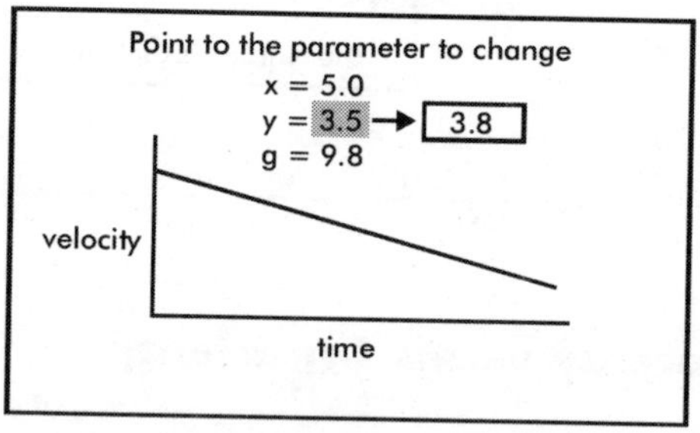

This automatically maintains the context: the current value is shown for comparison, and the location of the typing in and of itself indicates which parameter is being changed. Here absolute consistency is far less important than *adjacency*—placing new items adjacent to logically related items (though this, too, may be thought of as a form of consistency).

Consistency *versus* Variety

If you write a series of programs, try to maintain consistency of presentation across the series. Consistency of the main interaction aspects and notation is important, because it gives the user a framework and a context. However, a conflict can arise between the need for consistency and the need for variety. Consistency in the displays (and interactions) builds the user's confidence that he or she knows what to expect and how to use the materials. On the other hand, if every display is laid out exactly like every other display, the lack of variety can lead to boredom. One way to deal with this conflict is to provide strict consistency only at the highest level. For example, every programme should have a title page giving the names of the authors and their affiliations, and multi-part programs should have a table of contents. But the individual components inside the programme might vary a lot, with consistency provided in a general way (e.g., by drawing new display elements near the most recent display) rather than by using specific unvarying layouts.

Example

As an illustration of balancing the multiple issues in building a good interactive display, consider the following sequence of "snapshots" from a discussion of the relationship between pressure and volume for an ideal gas.

PV = nRT

The ideal gas law expresses the relationship between these variables

P	(Pressure)
V	(Volume)
N	(Number of moles)
T	(temperature)

For ideal gas

Note that context is maintained by the retention of the original equation at the top of the screen.

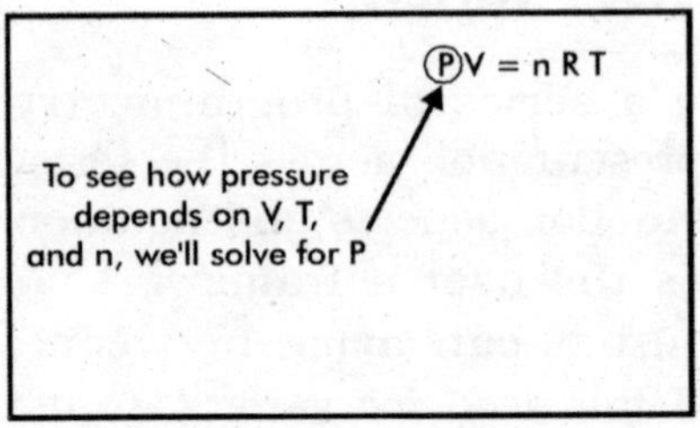

Important elements, and their connections, are highlighted temporarily; comments and explanations are presented, then removed.

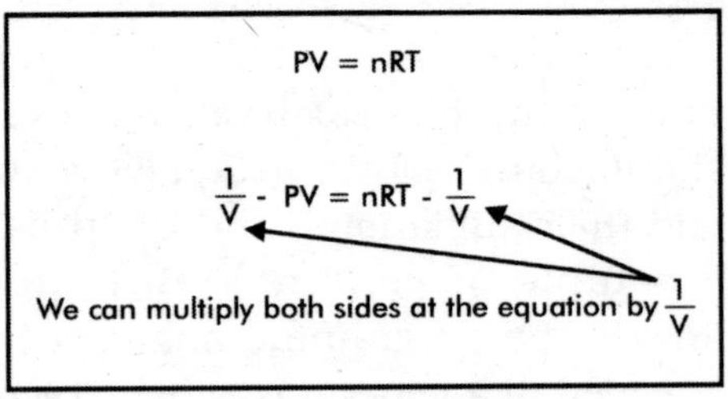

The step-by-step process makes it possible to check students' understanding along the way:

$$PV = nRT$$

$$P = \frac{nRT}{V}$$

If the volume decreases, will the pressure go up or down?

Note, too, that all of the displays are sparse and have plenty of empty space. Explanatory text is provided, then erased when it is no longer relevant to the current step. The sparseness of the displays makes it easy for the student to focus on the most important points in the discussion. Consider how the how cluttered the display would have been if all of the explanatory text had been left on the screen, and how cryptic the process would have been if no explanatory text had been used.

Interactivity

Designing interactive programs is surprisingly difficult and doesn't come naturally. It is very different from designing a book or a lecture, where there is very little interaction. It may be helpful to keep in mind the way you tutor an individual student or the way you run a very interactive small-group discussion session. Such interactive experiences may provide some ideas for interactive computer programs. There are, of course, some factors which are quite specific to the computer medium.

Perhaps the most generally useful guideline is, "Never tell when you can ask." For example, an author drew a distribution of points on a graph and wrote on the screen, "The average weight of this group of puppies is 3 pounds."

Avoid Typing

Bear in mind that typing is usually harder than pointing. Certainly there are many situations where it is appropriate or even necessary to require keyboard input. But every time you require the keyboard you should ask yourself whether there is an easier, more direct way to handle the interaction. Remember that most students are not skilled touch typists.

No Mouse?

A pointing device such as a mouse facilitates input to such an extent that it is practically a requirement for interactive programs. You may, however, need to work with older computers which do not have such a device. Many older programs incorporate quite successful schemes for using the keyboard to move a screen pointer. Typical approaches include using arrow keys or a key cluster such as "i j k m" to move a cursor, or using the space bar to cycle through possible selections on a menu or diagram. In situations where "pointing" input is important, using the keyboard in this fashion is much better than requiring extensive or complex typing.

Don't mix input modes

Avoid mixing keyboard and mouse actions for the same input. It can be quite annoying to have to move rapidly between two different input devices. This is a matter of consistency as well: stay with one or the other for a while.

Wait for the user

Don't use timed pauses (a pause for a specific amount of time) except for very special purposes such as animations. A common mistake is to display some text, pause three seconds, draw a graph, pause three seconds, then erase the entire screen in preparation for something else. This is disastrous. If the user glances out of the window, or sneezes, or is interrupted by a friend, the whole sequence may be missed. Even without that fatal full-screen erase, this kind of presentation is frustrating. Some users will wish that the pauses had been shorter. Other users will wish that the pauses had been longer. There may not exist one single individual (other than the author!) for whom the pauses are the right length. It is far better to wait for a signal from the user (typically a mouse click or a keypress) before moving on to the next item, thus making the display go at the user's own pace. Note the comparison with a lecture for a large group of students, where the lecture necessarily bores some students because it goes too slowly, and swamps other students for whom it goes too rapidly. There is no need to carry over this common source of frustration to an interactive medium.

Provide Instructions

In a research programme written and used only by yourself, little or no explanatory text is required because you know what the programme is supposed to do. But someone else might not be able to use the programme at all without an instruction manual. Since instruction manuals quickly get out of date as a programme is revised and are seldom around when one needs them, it is important that the programme be usable on its own, without a manual, which mandates that adequate instructions should be found in the programme itself. On the other hand, you should and can avoid excessive amounts of text. Long paragraphs telling the user what to do are much less effective than showing the user interactively what to do. Telling is ineffective because the user won't read long instructions and because it is difficult for the user to translate written instructions in one context into actions in a different context. Showing is direct and context specific, and it is possible because of the interactive and dynamic nature of the medium. Here are some specific suggestions for handling instructions:

- Provide instructions for a task as part of its display.
- Keep instructions terse and telegraphic.
- Show, don't tell, the user what to do.
- Step the user through a complex input sequence once.

On-screen Instructions

Ideally, instructions for user input should be on the display where the task is performed, not on an introductory page at the beginning of the programme. Before encountering the actual task, a user cannot digest or remember a long paragraph describing a sequence of operations or mechanisms for providing input. Do not expect a user to remember complex input conventions. Very frequently used control options are an exception; it is not only unnecessary to put "Press RETURN to go on" on every display, it is distracting and eventually even annoying.

Teach the Interface

If the interface has some unusual features, teach these features explicitly, in a step-by-step manner. Treat this as another teaching task: showing how to use an unusual interface should be just as interactive as teaching the content. Ask, don't tell. Have the user exercise the various options while your programme watches in detail. It is not adequate to discuss the interface conventions in several pages of passive text at the start of the programme. Such instructions will certainly not be remembered. If you are pressed for time and must nevertheless resort to mere textual description, at the very least don't forget to provide an easy mechanism for reviewing those instructions at a later time!

Input Analysis

Inputs must always be analyzed to see whether they are valid, and invalid inputs should be handled in a sensible way. This may sound obvious, but it is quite common for new authors to violate this rule. For example, suppose you let the user choose the initial speed and angle for a kicked football, and you then display the trajectory of the ball. You should normally tell the student what range of values your programme will handle; you definitely must check to make sure that the inputs are indeed within range. If you just blindly use whatever values are input, without checking their validity, the trajectory might go off the screen in a confusing way. In some situations, failing to check the input could even cause the programme to crash (e.g., trying to take the square root of a negative input value, when you were expecting a positive input.).

Basic Checks

Validity

First, check that the input is the kind you expect. If you ask for a number, you should first check to see that the input is a number, not some non-numerical word or sentence, or a numerical expression which is ill-formed (such as "3+*5–"). If you detect a mouse click, you should check to see whether the mouse cursor is indeed on a meaningful display object. What do you do if you find the input is invalid? To prevent frustration and confusion, you must provide immediate feedback to the user, stating why the input is not a valid one. For example, if the input is a number but not in the desired range, you can remind the user of the specified range restrictions and ask for different input. If the mouse click is in an inappropriate region, you can tell this to the user and reiterate or rephrase your instructions "That's not on the graph. Click on one of the curves on the graph."

Ignore Blank Inputs

Users frequently press the RETURN key accidentally before typing anything at a prompt. The consequences can be disastrous if the programme simply accepts this and proceeds to judge the response incorrect, assume a default value, or take some other action. Usually blank inputs should be ignored when typing is requested.

Verbal Input

As Culley eloquently describes, the machinery for analyzing free-form sentence inputs is massive, complex, and requires that the computer "know" a great deal about the specific context. Constructing such natural language understanding programs is still very much a research endeavor. Unless language itself is the focus of your programme, it is unlikely to be practical to provide this kind of resource. Lacking such intelligence, it is very difficult for a computer programme to analyze sentence inputs correctly, and one should avoid asking the student for words or sentences unless absolutely necessary. Nor is it appropriate to pretend or imply to the student that sentence input will be understood if it won't be, because this creates expectations which cannot be met. If asked for free-form input, the student will become very frustrated if it becomes apparent that the programme can't actually process free-form input. Even if the student is asked a yes/no question to be answered with a typed response, the programme had better be prepared for a wide range of inputs such as sure, yep, yeah, yup, I believe so, I think so, nope, etc. And what do you do with "I don't think so" or "maybe"? It is far better in this case to ask for a mouse click on a YES box or a NO box, or else to ask explicitly for "y" or "n" as the only acceptable typed response.

This is not to imply that sentence input is never appropriate. There are successful foreign-language sentence translation drills which do function quite well. But these drills have typically placed very tight constraints on the range of analyzable sentence forms, given the context of a particular lesson in a particular elementary course, where the student knows only a small vocabulary and only a few forms of syntax.

Allow Synonyms

Even for simple numeric or one-word answers, do try hard to accept a broad range of equivalent responses. If the input is a number, you should accept equivalent expressions (e.g., "30/6" should normally be taken as completely equivalent to 5, except in a drill on division). If the input is a word, try to accept its most common synonyms (e.g., "car, auto, automobile"). If a response is close to being acceptable, it is advisable to indicate this explicitly even if you are unwilling to accept this near miss. For example, if you want the student to identify "acetylene" and the student types "acetalene," it would be disastrous merely to say "You're wrong," because the student will then think that it isn't acetylene and will go off on a wrong track. You really should say something like "You have the right idea, but your spelling isn't quite right—please try to spell it in the standard form." Of course the ability to handle such near misses depends critically on the authoring tools available to you.

Feedback

Give Clear, Explicit Feedback

Students who believe they have understood what to do can become frustrated very quickly if their actions do not produce the results they expect. It is essential to provide feedback that makes it clear that the computer has detected input, and how the input has been interpreted.

Avoid Cuteness

In part because of a need for accuracy, in part because of the lack of clear emotional and personal context, it is important to avoid being cute. In our experience, it just doesn't work. It may have effects opposite to those you intend. Your personality will come through in your materials, just as it will if you write a book. Yet there are constraints imposed by the medium on how you can express that personality. Be polite and friendly, but avoid cuteness.

A related point is that one should avoid cute "rewards" in the form of lengthy unrelated graphics or music, especially if they recur often. After the third or fourth delay caused by having to sit through yet another irrelevant sequence of this kind, the user may be ready to scream. If short sounds are used only to augment other kinds of highlighting, offer the user an option to turn this off, so as not to disturb others when the materials are used in a public place.

Analyze for Misconceptions

Unfortunately, most input analysis problems are far more complex and subtle than the examples in the preceding section suggest. A particular "invalid" input may be indicative of an important misconception which should be dealt with extensively. As such, "invalid" inputs are not mere nuisances which need to be checked for, but critical indicators of student understanding to be used for guiding the following interaction. In some heavily algorithmic areas such as mathematics or science, the programme can often diagnose problems in a general way. For example, all numerical inputs can be checked for an overall sign error. Numbers resulting from division can be checked for inversion (4/3 instead of 3/4).

However, even with a precise diagnosis of a student's problem, there remains the pedagogical and motivational enigma of what to do about it. Should you immediately tell the student what the "right" answer is? Should the programme say "You're kind a on the right track, but have you considered such-and-such?" These problems arise when tutoring a student in person, and they arise when a computer is helping the student. The challenge must be faced somehow, even though there is little theory or practice to guide the attempt.

Avoid Dead Ends

One important guideline can be offered: Do not let the student get trapped in a blind alley, where he or she must answer a question in order to proceed but cannot find an input that is satisfactory to the programme. This is without a doubt the most frustrating aspect of poorly written materials. Often the underlying fault is a failure of the programme to accept alternative valid forms of the answer. But even if the student can't come up with a valid answer, the programme must provide some way to request help or to bypass the question, or at least to back up and review before trying again. If no other scheme seems feasible, at least provide some way for the student to request what the correct answer is. You might give increasingly detailed hints after each wrong response, until finally saying explicitly what you were looking for. Even with such an incremental scheme in place, you still might provide a way to see the correct answer without going through all those levels of hints.

No Browsing

It is tempting to provide an easy way to browse through a tutorial programme with essentially no effort, by letting the user just press RETURN in order to proceed without answering a question. This may be useful to an instructor who wants to get a quick overview of the material. It is rarely appropriate for students because it is undermines the interactivity which is the hallmark of good educational programs. We have even seen students complain about a browsing mode or easy help, claiming that it was the author's fault for allowing them to breeze through the material without paying attention or learning anything! There are other, more appropriate mechanisms for giving students control and allowing them to move about in a programme.

Test and Observe

Above all, because of the great difficulties of handling user input well, it is vitally important that you watch students using your programme, to see what kinds of difficulties they run into. Do not wait until your programme is "finished" to do this. Invite two or three students to go through your programme while you sit beside them taking notes. You will be utterly amazed the first time you do this. Student creativity in thinking up responses you hadn't imagined is limitless! After small-scale testing with two or three students and revision based on that testing, try automated collection of input from twenty or thirty students, if you have the appropriate computer tools to do this. Revise again based on this more extensive testing.

User Control

There are few things more frustrating to users of educational software than a feeling of lack of control over the programme. Angry students, trapped in sequences that they feel are inappropriate (too easy, too hard, confusing, irrelevant), are not receptive learners. As a teacher and author, you may in fact know better than your students what material they need to cover and in what order. However, it simply does not work to force students through a sequence of activities. You should make your overall plan clear with maps, suggestions, and reminders, but you must allow students to make choices of activities and to change their minds in the middle.

Books provide an analogy helpful for designing good user control. The author's overall plan and organization is clearly embodied in the sequence of chapters and the order of topics within a chapter of a book. The most natural course for the reader is simply to read the material in the order in which it occurs in the book. It is, however, possible to skip sections or whole chapters, to read them in a different order, to stop in the middle of a section and go back and review a previous section, and so on. Books provide tools to help readers make such choices: a table of contents, an index, and chapter headings on each page. Analogous maps and control options must be provided in educational computer activities as well.

Moving Around in the Programme

Give the user lots of control over the programme. One of the most important aspects of control is the ability to move around inside the programme—to be able to skip to a later section or to review an earlier section. In order to allow the user to exercise control, though, it is necessary to make clear both the current and overall context and location in the programme.

A multi-section programme might include displays like these:

- ❒ Title page (names and affiliations of the authors)
- ❒ Brief statement of purpose
- ❒ Table of contents
- ❒ Section 1 (displays marking transitions between sections)

❐ Section 2, etc.

Electronic Structure of Atoms
Part I

The Afbau Principle

Ruth Chabay
Department of Chemistry

The title page establishes the basic context and identifies who is responsible for the material.

Index
The Aufbau Principle
* 1. Purpose
* 2. Electrons
* 3. Energy levels, shells, & orbitals
4. The Aufbau Principle
5. Problems: The Aufbau Principle
6. d & f orbitals
7. Review Problems
Click on the the section you choose.
* Marks sections you have completed.

A table of contents provides transportation among sections of the programme and may also indicate student progress, reminding the student of what sections have already been completed. The student need only point to a section or type its number to go to the chosen section. Provide a menu or other well-advertised option to permit the user at any time to get to the table of contents.

PORPUSE of this lesson

In chemical reactions elections may be lost, gained, or shared by different chemical species.

In this lesson you will study the electronic structure of atoms. Knowing the electronic structure of an element allows us to predict many of its chemical properties.

A statement of purpose provides additional context and goals, and may also list prerequisites.

3. Energy levels, shells, & orbitals

Index

NEXT

In passing from one section into the next, indicate this with a characteristic section title, just as is done with chapters in a book. If you don't point out this transition between sections, the user has no sense of progress and flow.

Advertise Control Options

It is very important that control options be not only easy to use but obvious. Don't hide them, and don't expect that a single mention at the start is sufficient For example, getting back to the table of contents should at all times be a prominent menu option, a standard keypress, or even a little symbol on the screen to click on. Also consider offering easy options for moving forward or back within a section, to provide flexibility at all levels of the programme.

Use buttons rather than menus for frequently used options. A visible, onscreen control option such as a "button" (a square to click in) is often more appropriate than a hidden "menu" (a pull-down or pop-up list of options which must be specifically requested before becoming visible). The immediacy of a button, and the fact that buttons are typically small, often justifies taking up screen space for the option. Relegate to hidden menus only those options which are not used very often. On the other hand, do exercise judgement: don't clutter the screen with dozens of buttons.

Remove Inactive Control Options

Remove or visually deactivate (e.g., "gray out") any control options that have become inactive or are not relevant at this time, such as buttons, menu items, or reminders of control keys. Users invariably will try to make use of these options and will become frustrated or confused when they don't work.

Provide a way out

Bear in mind that changing one's mind is a user prerogative. Don't lock the user into something, even under user choice. For example, if a process will take a long time, such as plotting a complicated satellite orbit, be sure you provide and prominently advertise some method for stopping the process prematurely. It can be extremely frustrating to get into something and not be able to get out.

Make parameters available

We spoke earlier about checking for valid parameter values in a simulation. As far as the issue of control is concerned, it is important to make available as many of the parameters as possible for modification by the user (e.g., birth rates in a population projection programme). Be sure to display the current values, to give the user adequate context for changing them.

Where am I?

It is often difficult in the computer medium to have a good sense of where you are in the material, which leads to uneasiness and a feeling of lack of control. With a book, it is physically obvious when you are coming to the end, and it is quick and easy to flip a few pages and estimate where the end of the chapter is. The computer screen doesn't automatically give these visual cues, so they must be provided some other way. Even better than a usage-marked table of contents may be an easily accessible graphical "map" of the programme, indicating with boxes and arrows where the user is, where he or she may go.

Within a section, a local indicator is important. In a twenty-item drill on balancing chemical equations, be sure to display prominently "7 right, 13 to go," updating this message after every item.

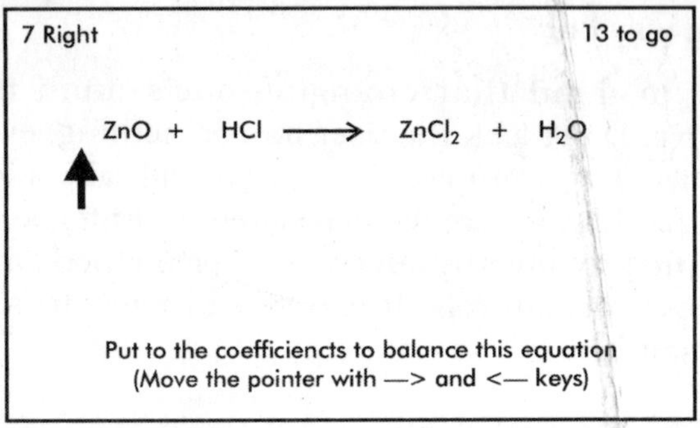

Note also in this example the blank space left for comments and feedback in the middle of the screen, and the avoidance of mixed input modes; all input, including cursor movement, is done with the keyboard.

Hints for Development

Explore the medium

A good way to get a feel for a new medium is to immerse oneself in existing examples. It is not enough to dip into instructional programs or to watch demonstrations. Work *completely* through some good instructional programs. Probably the vast majority of instructional programs are of poor quality, because the field is still so new. There do, however, exist good programs, and one can learn a great deal about the strengths and weaknesses of the medium by experiencing these programs directly. When trying out such a programme, don't just skim it, but put yourself as much as possible in the shoes of the students for whom it was designed, and go through the whole thing. Make mistakes and note how they are handled. Even with very good materials you are likely to find troublesome or even aggravating aspects, partly due to current limitations of the medium and partly due to limited understanding on the part of even the best and most experienced authors. When you write your own materials, remember the frustrations you experienced when playing student, and try to anticipate and overcome such feelings on the part of your users.

Try new instructional approaches

Some pedagogical approaches are better suited to the computer medium than others, and sometimes the new medium suggests completely new styles of pedagogy. Certainly the medium favors interactive approaches. Since it is often possible to show a dynamic effect rather than being constrained just to talk about it, you might preface a formal exposition with an interactive, qualitative overview of the topic. As with any medium, think critically about exactly what you hope students will learn from your materials, and go after these goals explicitly. For example, if you want the student to learn planning, teach this explicitly rather than leaving it to chance. Detailed feedback from student use can help determine whether the materials are sufficiently explicit.

Develop interactively

During development, try your programme and revise it very frequently, on a scale of minutes, not days or weeks. It is useful to make a few rough sketches of screen displays and flow of control before starting work, but try to do as much of the work as possible in an interactive manner. Treat the medium as plastic, and think of yourself as a sculptor. Try this, try that, discard this, follow up that. Since the medium is itself an interactive one, let its interactivity suggest things to you. An idea you wrote down on paper may turn out to be all wrong when you try it on the computer, yet in playing with the medium you may find a different twist which suits the medium very well. Be open to throwing away initial ideas and even sizable chunks of programming whenever experimenting with the medium suggests a better way.

Move from the specific to the general

Try very simple things first to see how they "feel" before investing a lot of effort in complex versions. The bigger an investment you have made, the less likely you are to admit to yourself that it isn't working out. A closely related point is that while very general procedures have great power, it is frequently prudent to start with specific, special-case schemes which can be implemented quickly and easily. Only after you are convinced that you are on the right track might you extract what is common to your several procedures and combine them into one general case. In some cases you may even find that there is no need later to replace your specific routines with a general one, and that using specific rather than general procedures offers useful variety and specificity.

Initial testing

As discussed earlier, do try out your experimental programme with a few students and revise it accordingly. Do this rather early, long before you have talked yourself into believing that your programme is wonderful and finished, because after that point it will be much more difficult to accept contrary evidence.

If students have difficulty with parts of the programme, try to change the programme, not the students. Experiment with ways to simplify control and interactions, add more background, or break tasks into smaller parts, rather than providing more and more detailed instructions on how to work around the program's shortcomings.

Later testing

After your programme has been through testing and actual use by real students, revise again to turn it into a finished product you would be proud to distribute to colleagues. Robustness is crucial at this stage: the programme should certainly not crash, and it should react well to varied kinds of usage and a wide range of observed inputs. A programme sufficiently robust for you is not necessarily robust enough for your students, and even that programme may not be sufficiently robust for someone else's students, who may have different backgrounds. Do take the time to be finicky about display details. Even a single unwanted dot on the screen due to faulty erasing can seem quite annoying or confusing to many people. Be sure to remove spelling errors and other typos. Failure to pay sufficient attention to such details can seriously mar an otherwise excellent product.

Be flexible

We hope that our suggestions will be helpful to you. We should admit that in our own work we have not always lived up to these guidelines. Moreover, we occasionally violate them deliberately. This is a new field, and experimentation should be encouraged, because no one knows precisely what works well in all cases.

Summary

We have emphasized the novelty of the highly interactive computer medium, with its own distinctive esthetic. The key issues a developer must address are in the areas of display, interactivity, input, and control. Creative use of the new capabilities may lead not just to improvements in education but possibly even to new kinds of education.

4

Computers: Social Revolution in Education

Introduction

Most of what the school teachers from 1897 would see when visiting an elementary school would be familiar. The desks and furniture in the classroom would appear about the same. They would be able to recognize a modern textbook as being similar to the books they used. Most of the techniques and methods employed by today's teachers would probably make sense to them, and would be related to things they might have done with students in their own classrooms.

Papert made the point that unlike the world of the operating room, the world of schooling has not changed in fundamental "ways that have altered its nature". The one new technology in the classroom, with the exception of a television set, with which the teachers from 1897 would be unfamiliar, would be a computer. Slide projectors would correspond to magic lanterns, a tape recorder or record player would be like a victrola, and an electric typewriter would be comparable with manual typewriters of their own era. A computer, however, would be totally new, unlike any technology they had ever seen before.

Brief History of Computing

Normally, we think of computers as having been introduced during the period following World War II. In fact, much of the theoretical underpinnings for contemporary computing come from the middle of the 19th century and the work of the English inventor an mathematician Charles Babbage.

In 1822, Babbage demonstrated a very limited mechanical binary computer to the Royal Astronomical Society in London. Known as the *Difference Engine,* it was followed by a more advanced machine called the *Analytical Engine.* Although theoretically sound, both machines were mechanically flawed. Even the most carefully machined gears and cogs were not precise enough to undertake massive calculations. Although Babbage's machine was functional, it would need electrical switching systems before it could work on a practical basis.

Augusta Ada Byron (1815-1852)

Augusta Ada Byron (1815-1852), more widely known as Ada Countess of Lovelace, is among the most famous figures in the history of computing. The daughter of the 19th-century English Poet Lord Byron, she was a gifted and largely self-taught mathematician. In 1833, when she was only 18 years old, she met the scientist and inventor Charles Babbage. Babbage, the inventor of the Difference Engine and the Analytical Engine, is widely considered to have created the first modern computer. Realizing Byron's talent, he asked her to assist him in his work. This eventually led to Byron publishing a set of notes in 1843 in Richard Taylor *Scientific Memoirs* series, which included a set of instructions for programming the Analytical Engine and speculations about its possible applications and use in mathematical computation, artificial intelligence, and music.

Byron's work is considered a major contribution to the development of modern computing. In 1980, the U.S. Department of Defense named a computing language "Ada" in her honour. The Ada Project (TAP), a World Wide Web site on women in computing, is also named after her.

Over 100 years passed before Babbage's ideas were used in electronic computational devices. Most experts would agree that the modern digital computer can trace its roots back to the 1930s and the work of Konrad Zuse, a young German engineer, who developed a simple computer using telephone switching devices that were capable of being programmed.

By 1946, the first general purpose computer electronic calculator was formally dedicated at the Moore School of Electrical Engineering at the University of Pennsylvania. The machine was designed to do ballistic calculations for the U.S. Army. It was known as the Electronic Numerical Integrator and Computer (ENIAC).

The ENIAC was made up of 18,000 vacuum tubes, 70,000 resistors, 10,000 capacitors, and 6,000 switches. The size of a double garage, this early computer worked only for brief periods because its vacuum tubes kept burning out. The logic chip in most watches today is a far more sophisticated calculating device than was the ENIAC.

Early computers were limited by the necessity of using vacuum tubes. In 1947, the transistor was invented by scientists at Bell Laboratories. A tiny sandwich of semi-conducting materials was created so that a small amount of current entering one end of the transistor could control a larger amount of current in another transistor. The practical result was the creation of a simple switching device that could be used to control the flow of electrons. Transistors were much smaller than vacuum tubes, they generated very little heat in comparison, were very cheap to manufacture, and, unlike vacuum tubes, rarely burned out.

Transistors made it possible to begin to make computers both smaller and more efficient. By the late 1950s, transistors were being etched onto tiny wafers of silicon. This quickly led to multiple transistors and connections being etched on single slivers of silicon. The creation of the microchip made it possible to put entire sections of a computer's memory, or logic system, onto a very small space. Microchip: a computer chip on which are etched the components of a computer's central processing unit.

By 1971, the microprocessor had been invented. Essentially, this involved placing a complete microprocessor an entire central processing unit on a single silicon chip. Computers could now be made that would rest on the tip of your finger, which using the technology of the ENIAC, would have been the size of a football field 25 years earlier.

The invention of the integrated circuit made possible the microcomputer, or personal computer. Computers no longer had to be assembled out of millions of different parts, but could be miniaturized and mass-produced as single "integrated" units. Machines that were better and more efficient than those that would have cost millions of dollars in the 1950s and 1960s were now available to many people at an affordable price.

The rapid evolution of computer technology is perhaps one of the most interesting aspects of the contemporary computer revolution. Machines that were only dreamed about 15 or 20 years ago are now available to private citizens for less than $2,000. What happens when computing power becomes so cheap and common? How does it affect the work of people, the use to which computers are put, and so on? Why is the introduction of inexpensive computing in our culture and society relevant for educators in the classroom?

The availability of inexpensive but powerful computing in our society, and in turn our schools and classrooms, means that many things are happening that were not possible even a few years ago. Migrant students going to school in one part of the country in one season are having their records follow them as their families move to another part of the country following the harvest. Rural schools with very small populations and limited resources are having students take advanced placement courses online. Teachers have productivity tools like word processors and classroom management systems to prepare lesson plans and keep records. Students are taking mass-administered intelligence and achievement tests that are being automatically scored. Individual uses of school Internet access are being tracked by school system administrators.

The Microcomputer Revolution

Today computers can be found in offices, in schools, and in many homes. They are changing not only the way we live and work, but possibly even the way we think.

Prior to 1974 there was no such thing as a personal computer. That was the year that MITS, a company in New Mexico, came up with the idea of selling a kit that made it possible to assemble a working computer. It was called an Altair 8800 and is widely considered to be the first personal computer. When purchased assembled, the Altair cost $621. If customers built it themselves, the cost was only $395. The Altair had lots of flashing lights and switches and a very small memory. It was difficult to use. Computers that were much easier to use were developed within a short time. The most important was the Apple.

The Apple was designed by a young engineer named Steven Wozniak. Wozniak worked as a designer for Hewlett-Packard, a giant computer and calculator company. During his spare time, Wozniak, or "Woz" as he is more commonly known, began to design his own personal computer. Much of the technology he used in the machine already existed. A lot that went into it, however, was totally new.

Wozniak was not very interested in being a businessperson. He built his first computers mostly just for the fun of it. His friend Steven Jobs convinced him that they could start their own company to sell computers. Jobs, who was a vegetarian, came up with the name Apple for their company. It was supposed to suggest that the machine was friendly and easy to use. The first Apple computers were sold to the public in 1978. They were built by Wozniak and Jobs in the garage of Jobs' parents' home and were an immediate success. The Apple quickly evolved into the Apple II, Apple II+, Apple IIE, and in 1985, the Apple IIGS. With the introduction of the Macintosh line of computers in 1984, Apple had become one of the leading computer companies in the world. Other companies quickly followed Apple's lead into the personal computing industry. Early manufacturers included Atari, Timex, Osborne, Texas Instruments, and IBM.

By 1982, nearly three million personal computers had been sold. Today, more computers are being bought each year than televisions. Besides business and educational uses, they are coming into widespread use for entertainment and communication.

The history of computer science began long before the modern discipline of computer science that emerged in the twentieth century, and hinted at in the centuries prior. The progression, from mechanical inventions and mathematical theories towards the modern concepts and machines, formed a major academic field and the basis of a massive worldwide industry.

Early Computation

The earliest known tool for use in computation was the abacus, and it was thought to have been invented in Babylon circa 2400 BCE. Its original style of usage was by lines drawn in sand with pebbles. This was the first known computer and most advanced system of calculation known to date -

preceding Greek methods by 2,000 years. Abaci of a more modern design are still used as calculation tools today.

In 1115 BCE, the South Pointing Chariot was invented in ancient China. It was the first known geared mechanism to use a differential gear, which was later used in analog computers. The Chinese also invented a more sophisticated abacus from around the 2nd century BCE, known as the Chinese abacus.

In the 5th century BCE in ancient India, the grammarian Panini formulated the grammar of Sanskrit in 3959 rules known as the Ashtadhyayi which was highly systematized and technical. Panini used metarules, transformations and recursions.

The Antikythera mechanism is believed to be the earliest known mechanical analog computer. It was designed to calculate astronomical positions. It was discovered in the Antikythera wreck off the Greek island of Antikythera, between Kythera and Crete, and has been dated to *circa* 100 BC. Technological artifacts of similar complexity did not reappear until the 14th century, when mechanical astronomical clocks appeared in Europe.

Mechanical analog computing devices appeared again a thousand years later in the medieval Islamic world. Examples of devices from this period include the equatorium by Arzachel, the mechanical geared astrolabe by Abû Rayhân al-Bîrûnî, and the torquetum by Jabir ibn Aflah. Muslim engineers built a number of Automata, including some musical automata that could be 'programmed' to play different musical patterns. These devices were developed by the Banû Mûsâ brothers and Al-Jazari Muslim mathematicians also made important advances in cryptography, such as the development of cryptanalysis and frequency analysis by Alkindus.

When John Napier discovered logarithms for computational purposes in the early 17th century, there followed a period of considerable progress by inventors and scientists in making calculating tools. Around 1640, Blaise Pascal, a leading French mathematician, constructed the first mechanical adding device based on a design described by Greek mathematician Hero of Alexandria.

None of the early computational devices were really computers in the modern sense, and it took considerable advancement in mathematics and theory before the first modern computers could be designed.

Algorithms

In the 7th century, Indian mathematician Brahmagupta gave the first explanation of the Hindu-Arabic numeral system and the use of zero as both a placeholder and a decimal digit.

Approximately around the year 825, Persian mathematician Al-Khwarizmi wrote a book, *On the Calculation with Hindu Numerals*, that was principally responsible for the diffusion of the Indian system of numeration in the Middle East and then Europe. Around the 12th century, there was translation of this book written into Latin: *Algoritmi de numero Indorum*. These books presented newer concepts to perform a series of steps in order to accomplish a task such as the systematic application of arithmetic to algebra. By derivation from his name, we have the term algorithm. Algorithm-is the computer in using a mathematical equation.

Binary Logic

Around the 3rd century BC, Indian mathematician Pingala discovered the binary numeral system. This system, still used today in all modern computers, a sequence of ones and zeros can represent any number.

In 1703, Gottfried Leibnitz developed logic in a formal, mathematical sense with his writings on the binary numeral system. In his system, the ones and zeros also represent *true* and *false* values or *on* and *off* states. But it took more than a century before George Boole published his Boolean Algebra in 1854 with a complete system that allowed computational processes to be mathematically modelled.

By this time, the first mechanical devices driven by a binary pattern had been invented. The industrial revolution had driven forward the mechanization of many tasks, and this included weaving. Punched cards controlled Joseph Marie Jacquard's loom in 1801, where a hole punched in the card indicated a binary *one* and an unpunched spot indicated a binary *zero*. Jacquard's loom was far from being a computer, but it did illustrate that machines could be driven by binary systems.

Birth of Computer Science

Before the 1920s, *computers* (sometimes *computors*) were human clerks that performed computations. They were usually under the lead of a physicist. Many thousands of computers were employed in commerce, government, and research establishments. Most of these computers were women, and they were known to have a degree in calculus. Some performed astronomical calculations for calendars.

After the 1920s, the expression *computing machine* referred to any machine that performed the work of a human computer, especially those in accordance with effective methods of the Church-Turing thesis. The thesis states that a mathematical method is effective if it could be set out as a list of instructions able to be followed by a human clerk with paper and pencil, for as long as necessary, and without ingenuity or insight.

Machines that computed with continuous values became known as the *analog* kind. They used machinery that represented continuous numeric quantities, like the angle of a shaft rotation or difference in electrical potential.

Digital machinery, in contrast to analog, were able to render a state of a numeric value and store each individual digit. Digital machinery used difference engines or relays before the invention of faster memory devices.

The phrase *computing machine* gradually gave away, after the late 1940s, to just *computer* as the onset of electronic digital machinery became common. These computers were able to perform the calculations that were performed by the previous human clerks.

Since the values stored by digital machines were not bound to physical properties like analog devices, a logical computer, based on digital equipment, was able to do anything that could be described "purely mechanical." The theoretical Turing Machine, created by Alan Turing, is a hypothetical device theorized in order to study the properties of such hardware.

Emergence of a Discipline

The Theoretical Groundwork

The mathematical foundations of modern computer science began to be laid by Kurt Gödel with his incompleteness theorem. In this theorem, he showed that there were limits to what could be proved and disproved within a formal system. This led to work by Gödel and others to define and describe these formal systems, including concepts such as mu-recursive functions and lambda-definable functions.

1936 was a key year for computer science. Alan Turing and Alonzo Church independently, and also together, introduced the formalization of an algorithm, with limits on what can be computed, and a "purely mechanical" model for computing.

These topics are covered by what is now called the Church–Turing thesis, a hypothesis about the nature of mechanical calculation devices, such as electronic computers. The thesis claims that any calculation that is possible can be performed by an algorithm running on a computer, provided that sufficient time and storage space are available.

Turing also included with the thesis a description of the Turing machine. A Turing machine has an infinitely long tape and a read/write head that can move along the tape, changing the values along the way. Clearly such a machine could never be built, but nonetheless, the model can simulate the computation of any algorithm which can be performed on a modern computer.

Turing is so important to computer science that his name is also featured on the Turing Award and the Turing test. He contributed greatly to British code-breaking successes in the Second World War, and continued to design computers and software through the 1940s, but committed suicide in 1954.

At a symposium on large-scale digital machinery in Cambridge, Turing said, "We are trying to build a machine to do all kinds of different things simply by programming rather than by the addition of extra apparatus".

In 1948, the first practical computer that could run stored programs, based on the Turing machine model, had been built—the Manchester Baby.

In 1950, Britain's National Physical Laboratory completed Pilot ACE, a small scale programmable computer, based on Turing's philosophy.

Shannon and Information Theory

Up to and during the 1930s, electrical engineers were able to build electronic circuits to solve mathematical and logic problems, but most did so in an *ad hoc* manner, lacking any theoretical rigor. This changed with Claude Elwood Shannon's publication of his 1937 master's thesis, A Symbolic Analysis of Relay and Switching Circuits. While taking an undergraduate philosophy class, Shannon had been exposed to Boole's work, and recognized that it could be used to arrange electromechanical relays (then used in telephone routing switches) to solve logic problems. This concept, of utilizing the properties of electrical switches to do logic, is the basic concept that underlies all electronic digital computers, and his thesis became the foundation of practical digital circuit design when it became widely known among the electrical engineering community during and after World War II.

Shannon went on to found the field of information theory with his 1948 paper titled A Mathematical Theory of Communication, which applied probability theory to the problem of how to best encode the information a sender wants to transmit. This work is one of the theoretical foundations for many areas of study, including data compression and cryptography.

Wiener and Cybernetics

From experiments with anti-aircraft systems that interpreted radar images to detect enemy planes, Norbert Wiener coined the term cybernetics from the Greek word for "steersman." He published "Cybernetics" in 1948, which influenced artificial intelligence. Wiener also compared computation, computing machinery, memory devices, and other cognitive similarities with his analysis of brain waves.

Information Technology in India

The Indian Information Technology industry accounts for a 5.9% of the country's GDP and export earnings as of 2009, while providing employment to a significant number of its tertiary sector workforce. More than 2.3 million people are employed in the sector either directly or indirectly, making it one of the biggest job creators in India and a mainstay of the national economy. In March 2009, annual revenues from outsourcing operations in India amounted to US$60 billion and this is expected to increase to US$225 billion by 2020. The most prominent IT hub is IT capital Bangalore. The other emerging destinations are Chennai, Hyderabad, Mumbai, Pune, NCR, Jaipur and Kolkata. Technically proficient immigrants from India sought jobs in the western world from the 1950s onwards as India's education system produced more engineers than its industry could absorb. India's growing stature in the information age enabled it to form close ties with both the United States of America and the European Union.

India's IT Services industry was born in Mumbai in 1967 with the establishment of Tata Group in partnership with Burroughs. The first software export zone SEEPZ was set-up here way back in 1973, the old avatar of the modern day IT park. More than 80 percent of the country's software exports happened out of SEEPZ in 80s.

Each year India produces roughly 500,000 engineers in the country, out of them only 25% to 30% possessed both technical competency and English language skills, although 12% of India's population can speak in English. India developed a number of outsourcing companies specializing in customer support via Internet or telephone connections. By 2009, India also has a total of 37,160,000 telephone lines in use, a total of 506,040,000 mobile phone connections, a total of 81,000,000 Internet users comprising 7.0% of the country's population, and 7,570,000 people in the country have access to broadband Internet making it the 12th largest country in the world in terms of broadband Internet users. Total fixed-line and wireless subscribers reached 543.20 million as of November, 2009.

Formative Years (Till 1991)

The Indian Government acquired the EVS EM computers from the Soviet Union, which were used in large companies and research laboratories. In 1968 Tata Consultancy Services established in SEEPZ, Mumbai by the Tata Group were the country's largest software producers during the

1960s. As an outcome of the various policies of Jawaharlal Nehru (office: 15 August 1947 – 27 May 1964) the economically beleaguered country was able to build a large scientific workforce, second in numbers only to that of the United States of America and the Soviet Union. On 18 August 1951 the Minister of education Maulana Abul Kalam Azad, inaugurated the Indian Institute of Technology at Kharagpur in West Bengal. Possibly modelled after the Massachusetts Institute of Technology these institutions were conceived by a 22 member committee of scholars and entrepreneurs under the chairmanship of N.R. Sarkar.

Relaxed immigration laws in the United States of America (1965) attracted a number of skilled Indian professionals aiming for research. By 1960 as many as 10,000 Indians were estimated to have settled in the US. Kapur. By the 1980s a number of engineers from India were seeking employment in other countries. In response, the Indian companies realigned wages to retain their experienced staff. In the *Encyclopedia of India*, Kamdar reports on the role of Indian immigrants (1980 - early 1990s) in promoting technology-driven growth:

The National Informatics Centre was established in March 1975. The inception of The Computer Maintenance Company (CMC) followed in October 1976. Between 1977-1980 the country's Information Technology companies Tata Infotech, Patni Computer Systems, and Wipro, had become visible. The 'microchip revolution' of the 1980s had convinced both Indira Gandhi and her successor Rajiv Gandhi that electronics and telecommunications were vital to India's growth and development. MTNL underwent technological improvements. Between 1986-1987, the Indian government embarked upon the creation of three wide-area computer networking schemes: INDONET (intended to serve the IBM mainframes in India), NICNET (the network for India's National Informatics Centre), and the academic research oriented Education and Research Network (ERNET).

1991–2001

Regulated VSAT links became visible in 1985. Desai (2006) describes the steps taken to relax regulations on linking in 1991:

Videsh Sanchar Nigam Limited (VSNL) introduced Gateway Electronic Mail Service in 1991, the 64 kbit/s leased line service in 1992, and commercial Internet access on a visible scale in 1992. Election results were displayed via National Informatics Centre's NICNET.

The Indian economy underwent economic reforms in 1991, leading to a new era of globalization and international economic integration. Economic growth of over 6% annually was seen between 1993-2002. The economic reforms were driven in part by significant the internet usage in the country. The new administration under Atal Bihari Vajpayee—which placed the development of Information Technology among its top five priorities formed the Indian National Task Force on Information Technology and Software Development.

Wolcott & Goodman report on the role of the Indian National Task Force on Information Technology and Software Development:

> The New Telecommunications Policy, 1999 helped further liberalize India's telecommunications sector. The Information Technology Act 2000 created legal procedures for electronic transactions and e-commerce.

Throughout the 1990s, another wave of Indian professionals entered the United States. The number of Indian Americans reached 1.7 million by 2000. This immigration consisted largely of highly educated technologically proficient workers. Within the United States, Indians fared well in science, engineering, and management. Graduates from the Indian Institutes of Technology (IIT) became known for their technical skills. The success of Information Technology in India not only had economic repercussions but also had far-reaching political consequences. India's reputation both as a source and a destination for skilled workforce helped it improve its relations with a number of world economies. The relationship between economy and technology—valued in the western world facilitated the growth of an entrepreneurial class of immigrant Indians, which further helped aid in promoting technology-driven growth.

2001–present

India is now one of the biggest IT capitals in the modern world.

The economic effect of the technologically inclined services sector in India—accounting for 40% of the country's GDP and 30% of export earnings as of 2006, while employing only 25% of its workforce

Today, Bangalore is known as the Silicon Valley of India and contributes 33% of Indian IT Exports. India's second and third largest software companies are head-quartered in Bangalore, as are many of the global SEI-CMM Level 5 Companies.

And Mumbai too has its share of IT companies once that are established as well as start-ups, and these include Reliance, TCS, Patni, LnT Infotech, i-Flex, WNS, Shine, Naukri, Jobspert etc. and these IT and dot com companies are ruling the roost of Mumbai's relatively high octane industry of Information Technology.

Such is the growth in investment and outsourcing, it was revealed that Cap Gemini will soon have more staff in India than it does in its home market of France with 21,000 personnel+ in India.

On 25 June 2002 India and the European Union agreed to bilateral cooperation in the field of science and technology. A joint EU-India group of scholars was formed on 23 November 2001 to further promote joint research and development. India holds observer status at CERN while a joint India-EU Software Education and Development Center is due at Bangalore.

India's IT industry (USD bn)

India's IT industry (USD bn)				
Particulars	**FY 2004**	**FY 2005**	**FY 2006**	**FY 2007E**
IT Services	10.4	13.5	17.8	23.7
• *Exports*	7.3	10.0	13.13	18.1
• *Domestic*	3.1	3.5	4.5	5.6
ITES-BPO	3.4	5.2	7.2	9.5
• *Exports*	3.1	4.6	6.3	8.3
• *Domestic*	0.3	0.6	0.9	1.2
Engineering services, R&D and Software products	2.9	3.9	5.3	6.5
• *Exports*	2.5	3.1	4.0	4.9
• *Domestic*	0.4	0.7	1.3	1.6
Hardware	5.0	5.9	7.0	8.2
Total IT industry	21.6	28.4	37.4	47.8
• *Exports*	13.4	18.2	24.1	31.9
• *Domestic*	8.3	10.2	13.2	15.9

Top Seven IT Hubs in India

Ranking	**City/Region**	**Description**
1	Bangalore	Popularly known as the capital of the Silicon Valley of India is currently leading in Information Technology Industries in India.
2	Chennai	It is also called as India's second silicon valley. With better infrastructure and manpower Chennai is likely to beat Bangalore out of its title in the coming years.
3	Hyderabad	Hyderabad which has good infrastructure and good government support is also a good technology base in India.

4	Pune	Pune, a major industrial town, hosts numerous multinational and national software giants along with BPO and KPO firms. World class SEZs like Hinjawadi IT park and Magarpatta city give Pune a distinct advantage. The city is a major educational hub and churns out thousands of technocrats every year.
5	Kolkata	Kolkata which is slowly becoming a major IT hub in near future. Some of the well known technological corporations are establishing their centres in Kolkata.
6	NCR	The National Capital Region of India comprising Delhi, Gurgaon, Faridabad, Noida, Greater Noida and Ghaziabad are having ambitious projects and are trying to do every possible thing for this purpose.
7	Mumbai	Popularly known as the commercial, entertainment, financial capital of India, This is one city that has seen tremendous growth in IT and BPO industry, it recorded 63% growth in 2008. TCS, Patni, LnT Infotech, I-Flex WNS and other companies are headquartered here.

Parallels between the Gutenberg and the Contemporary Computer Revolution

There are many parallels between the invention of printing and the growth and development of micro computing since the late 1970s. As per author, "the changes that are beginning to emerge in our world as a result of the large-scale introduction of microcomputers parallel many of the changes that took place in Europe as a consequence of the information revolution that followed the invention of printing".

Because of the high cost of mainframe computing up until the late 1970s, the machines and their programs were limited to a highly select group within the culture. Basically, only large corporations, selected academics, the government, and the military had access to computers.

The introduction of micro, or personal, computers democratized computing. It became available to almost anyone. Computer literacy is, in turn, an increasingly important issue because such a large number of people have access to the machines.

Just as the invention of printing took the writing and production of books out of the almost exclusive control of the universities and the church and put it into the hands of the individual, the personal computer has moved computing out of the largely exclusive control of groups (e.g., the government and large corporations) and into the hands of private individuals.

Many factors have contributed to this phenomenon. In recent years, computers, like early books, have become easier to read and use, cheaper to buy, and more portable. Like books during the Renaissance and Reformation, which were originally written in Latin but began to be published in vernacular languages such as English, French, and Italian, computers have become increasingly "user friendly." Icons symbolic representations of complex programme groups — are used to simplify the use of computers. As the cost of computers has gone down, there has been a corresponding expansion in their use. In the context of the invention of modern printing and the Gutenberg revolution, the significance of portability can be seen in the comments of

Lucien Febvre and Henri-Jean Martin, who argued that "thanks to printing and the multiplication of texts, the book ceased to seem a precious object to be consulted in a library: there was more and more need to be able to carry it about readily in order to refer to it or read it at any time". Precisely the same thing has happened with computers.

Computers that are more powerful than the largest mainframe machines of the 1950s are now carried as electronic calendars and pocket organizers, and laptop computers with the power of scientific workstations from the late 1980s can be carried into the classroom or on business trips.

Desktop Publishing: involves the use of computers to create text and graphics for the production of pamphlets, newsletters and books.

New technologies of this sort, whether the book or the personal computer, have an enormous potential to empower individuals. Martin Luther was able to supersede the censorship and control of the medieval Catholic Church because he had the power of the printing press to disseminate his ideas. To what extent is the computer, in manifestations such as the Internet and desktop publishing, a similarly empowering technology?

Gutenberg and the contemporary computer revolution relevant for educators in the classroom

The introduction of movable type made it possible to create inexpensive, highly detailed books. By the middle of the 17th century a new form of educational media called the *textbook* was created. Curriculum materials were standardized. Writers, illustrators, and publishers devoted themselves to the creation of standard texts.

The textbook created a new learning or instructional space. Likewise, the computer in our own era is creating a new type of learning space. CD-ROM discs with hypermedia programs for reading include passages where students click on a word and have a definition appear. Students also have access to files that read aloud to them. This is happening in multiple languages with illustrated animations as well as many other features.

Beyond the chalkboard, presentation systems such as Powerpoint and Astound are available through the computer. Encyclopedias are no longer print volume texts. They are now either interactive CD-ROMs or online sources on the Internet and the World Wide Web. Record keeping for the teacher has moved from the grade book to electronic grading and management programs.

The Computer as a "Singularity"

According to the science fiction writer Vernor Vinge:

> When a race succeeds in making creatures that are smarter than it is, then all the rules are changed. And from the standpoint of that race, you've gone through a Singularity. That's because it's not possible before that point to talk meaningfully about the issues that are important after that point.

The computer, as it has evolved from its mainframe origins in the 1940s and 1950s, may very well be a singularity that has changed the rules of our culture and society.

Knowledge and our ways of knowing are redefined by the computer in much the same way that the invention of the book changed the fundamental nature and meaning of learning during the Renaissance. Memory and recitation were no longer as important with the book as they were prior to its invention. Knowledge could be precisely reproduced. With the precision provided by the printing press, thousands of copies of exactly the same book could be reproduced without the fear of variant editions being created through the errors of scribes or copyists.

Having highly accurate texts is critical to the development of modern science. The ability to produce precise scientific drawings is equally important. Imagine not having the precision of the printing press to produce these types of publications. What would maps be like if they had to be drawn rather than printed? Imagine how the world would be different if everything you used in a book format was copied by hand rather than being mass-produced.

The computer, in a similar way, changes how we know and understand the world around us. We can create simulations of how things look when they move at the speed of light, we can organize huge amounts of data and retrieve them with relative ease, we can do complex mathematical computations that would take tens of thousands of hours to do by hand, and we can communicate instantaneously with people around the world.

We believe this type of shift in our ability to process information is in fact a singularity, just as the introduction of modern printing was a singularity at the end of the 15th century a singularity of profound social and cultural significance.

Why is the idea of the computer being a "Singularity" a relevant issue for educators in the classroom?

Mouse: a pointing device that allows the user to input commands into a computer.

The invention of movable type was a Singularity. As already noted, textbooks were a direct outcome of the invention of movable type. Before movable type and the textbook, neither teachers nor students regularly had books in their classrooms. Books were in libraries to be consulted by scholars. During the Middle Ages, teachers taught about what was in books. With the introduction of inexpensive printing as a Singularity, the nature of teaching changed with teachers and students having easy access to books in their classrooms. The introduction of wide access to the Internet and the World Wide Web may represent a similar Singularity affecting classroom practice. Teachers and students are no longer limited to the reference sources in their classroom or school. The Singularity of computers provides much easier access to the world's knowledge and thus is redefining recent traditions of instruction.

The Computer as 'Augmenting' Intelligence

Scanner. a device that uses a light sensitive reader to transform text or images into a digital signal that can be used by a computer. Scanning refers to the process of using a scanner.

Douglas C. Engelbart wrote a prophetic essay entitled "A Conceptual Framework for the Augmentation of Man's Intellect". He outlined the basic principles of word processing, the use of icon systems for computers, as well as ideas such as the computer mouse and digital scanning.

Augment Intelligence: To Supplement, Enhance or Support Intelligence

Engelbart also postulated that the computer could "augment," or enhance, the intelligence of its users. He described this process as augmenting man's intellect": "By 'augmenting man's intellect' we mean increasing the capability of a man to approach a complex problem situation, gain comprehension to suit his particular needs, and to derive solutions to problems". According to Engelbart, learning and understanding were naturally facilitated by using the computer. Better solutions to problems could be produced as well. The computer would also make it possible to be more accurate.

Engelbart talked, for example, about how using a computer as a word processor changes the entire process of composing a text:

> For instance, trial drafts can rapidly be composed from rearranged excerpts of old drafts, together with new words or passages which you insert by hand typing. Your first draft may represent a free outpouring of thoughts in any order, with the

inspection of foregoing thoughts continuously stimulating new considerations and ideas to be entered.

Ideas can be reordered, and new ideas can be integrated more easily. More complex procedures can be introduced into the process.

Using a word processor is not just a means to more efficient typing. What Engelbart argued is that it changes the actual process of writing. Besides allowing writers to continually revise their ideas, the computer allows them to check spelling and even grammar.

Douglas Engelbart—Computing Pioneer

Douglas Engelbart is among the most important figures in the history of contemporary computing. Yet he remains a relatively obscure figure — one known largely by experts in computing. Engelbart is most famous for having invented the computer mouse, display editing, windows, cross-file editing, outline processing, hypermedia, and groupware. Working out of the Augmentation Research Center at Stanford Research Institute, which he founded in 1963, Engelbart's work has focused around the issue of using technology to augment individual and collective intelligence. His ideas were originally developed for mainframe computers and only fully came to fruition with the development of personal computers and the Internet.

Recently, with the help of Sun Microsystems and Netscape Communications, Engelbart has been working to create alliances between business, government, and civic organizations. At the heart of this alliance is the concept of *bootstrapping*, an idea drawn from engineering in which the results of an action are fed back to achieve greater results more quickly with less effort.

As director of the Bootstrap Institute, Englebat and the institute's purpose is to "Boost" the "Collective IQ." According to Engelbart, "the Collective IQ of a group is a function of how quickly and intelligently it can respond to a situation.

This goes well beyond getting more information faster, to include leveraging its collective memory, perception, planning, reasoning, foresight, and experience into applicable knowledge. Such knowledge includes not only the captured knowledge products, such as documentation, plans, and source code, but also the accumulating 'web' of issues, lessons learned, rationale, commentary, dialog records, intelligence sources, and so on that iterate throughout the life-cycle of a project or situation".

Engelbart's ideas about collective IQ are still largely untested. His remarkable insights thus far in his career would tend to suggest that these new ideas are worth very careful attention and consideration.

Spell Checker. Software that checks for spelling errors. Typically part of word processing, software.

This is more important than it may seem. When using a spell checker in a word processing programme the effect is that the product will have what is essentially excellent or even perfect spelling. This type of tool changes the character of our writing and what we can achieve as individuals in terms of many aspects of the written word.

Engelbart's augmentation model has profound social and cultural implications. As Terry Winograd and Fernando Flores argued:

> All new technologies develop within the background of a tacit understanding of human nature and human work. The use of technology in turn leads to fundamental changes in what we do, and ultimately in what it is to be human. We encounter the deep questions of design when we recognize that in designing tools we are designing (ways of being).

In the case of Engelbart's ideas, the computer is not just a tool for efficiency, but a tool that literally changes our ways of organizing and interpreting the world. Like the invention of the telescope and the microscope in the 17th century, which opened new ways of knowing and understanding and functionally gave us a greater and more comprehensive vision, the computer has literally expanded our capacity to understand and interpret the world. In this context, the computer represents a revolutionary intellectual and social tool one that is as important as the inventions which made possible the scientific revolution of the late Renaissance and early modern periods.

Why is the augmentation of intelligence through computers a relevant issue for educators in the classroom?

Accurate spelling, the careful use of grammar, and precise calculation have always been important issues in education. Without them we cannot communicate well through writing, or work in mathematics or science. Arguments have recently arisen that students should use spelling and grammar checking systems to help them write, and use calculators or computers to do mathematical calculations. Some purists are horrified by this technological trend. If using a mechanical device like a computer to augment our ability to calculate, spell, or avoid a split infinitive is a bad educational practice, then is it likewise a bad practice to use a directory to look up a word and how to spell it? What basics do students need to learn? When should they use the computer to augment their intelligence, but not limit their abilities to think critically or solve problems? How does the use of the computer change what we need to teach and learn?

What happens when we can create a visualization model of what an object looks like at the speed of light? What happens when we can call up from our desktops virtually any of the great libraries of the world? What happens when we can manipulate words and images on the screen in ways that can only be described as a new type of electronic writing? How has the world changed?

Shakespeare *The Tempest* has a character that reflects on the "brave new world" now surrounding them. As educators, we have entered a brave new world of computing involving new ways of knowing and new types of intelligence.

It is a world full of many possibilities and fraught with many potential problems. How does the computer change the nature of learning and of knowing? What new meanings can be discovered with these machines and their software? How can they contribute to our work as educators?

❑❑❑

5

Computer Network

Introduction

A computer network allows sharing of resources and information among devices connected to the network. The Advanced Research Projects Agency (ARPA) funded the design of the Advanced Research Projects Agency Network (ARPANET) for the United States Department of Defense. It was the first operational computer network in the world. Development of the network began in 1969, based on designs developed during the 1960s. For a history see ARPANET, the first network.

Purpose

- *Facilitating communications.* Using a network, people can communicate efficiently and easily via e-mail, instant messaging, chat rooms, telephony, video telephone calls, and videoconferencing.
- *Sharing hardware.* In a networked environment, each computer on a network can access and use hardware

on the network. Suppose several personal computers on a network each require the use of a laser printer. If the personal computers and a laser printer are connected to a network, each user can then access the laser printer on the network, as they need it.

- *Sharing files, data, and information.* In a network environment, any authorized user can access data and information stored on other computers on the network. The capability of providing access to data and information on shared storage devices is an important feature of many networks.
- *Sharing software.* Users connected to a network can access application programs on the network.

Network Classifcation

The following list presents categories used for classifying networks.

Connection Method

Computer networks can be classified according to the hardware and software technology that is used to interconnect the individual devices in the network, such as optical fiber, Ethernet, Wireless LAN, HomePNA, Power line communication or G.hn.

Ethernet uses physical wiring to connect devices. Frequently deployed devices include hubs, switches, bridges and/or routers. Wireless LAN technology is designed to connect devices without wiring. These devices use radio waves or infrared signals as a transmission medium. ITU-T G.hn technology uses existing home wiring (coaxial cable, phone lines and power lines) to create a high-speed (up to 1 Gigabit/s) local area network.

Wired Technologies

- *Twisted pair wire* is the most widely used medium for telecommunication. Twisted-pair wires are ordinary telephone wires which consist of two insulated copper wires twisted into pairs and are used for both voice and data transmission. The use of two wires twisted together helps to reduce crosstalk and electromagnetic induction. The transmission speed ranges from 2 million bits per second to 100 million bits per second.

- *Coaxial cable* is widely used for cable television systems, office buildings, and other worksites for local area networks. The cables consist of copper or aluminium wire wrapped with insulating layer typically of a flexible material with a high dielectric constant, all of which are surrounded by a conductive layer. The layers of insulation help minimize interference and distortion. Transmission speed range from 200 million to more than 500 million bits per second.
- *Optical fibre cable* consists of one or more filaments of glass fibre wrapped in protective layers. It transmits light which can travel over extended distances without signal loss. Fibre-optic cables are not affected by electromagnetic radiation. Transmission speed may reach trillions of bits per second. The transmission speed of fibre optics is hundreds of times faster than for coaxial cables and thousands of times faster than for twisted-pair wire.

Wireless Technologies

- *Terrestrial Microwave:* Terrestrial microwaves use Earth-based transmitter and receiver. The equipment look similar to satellite dishes. Terrestrial microwaves use low-gigahertz range, which limits all communications to line-of-sight. Path between relay stations spaced approx. 30 miles apart. Microwave antennas are usually placed on top of buildings, towers, hills, and mountain peaks.

- *Communications Satellites:* The satellites use microwave radio as their telecommunications medium which are not deflected by the Earth's atmosphere. The satellites are stationed in space, typically 22,000 miles (for geosynchronous satellites) above the equator. These Earth-orbiting systems are capable of receiving and relaying voice, data, and TV signals.
- *Cellular and PCS Systems:* Use several radio communications technologies. The systems are divided to different geographic area. Each area has low-power transmitter or radio relay antenna device to relay calls from one area to the next area.
- *Wireless LANs:* Wireless local area network use a high-frequency radio technology similar to digital cellular and a low-frequency radio technology. Wireless LANs use spread spectrum technology to enable communication between multiple devices in a limited area. An example of open-standards wireless radio-wave technology is IEEE 802.11b.
- *Bluetooth:* A short range wireless technology. Operate at approx. 1Mbps with range from 10 to 100 meters. Bluetooth is an open wireless protocol for data exchange over short distances.
- *The Wireless Web:* The wireless web refers to the use of the World Wide Web through equipments like cellular phones, pagers, PDAs, and other portable communications devices. The wireless web service offers anytime/anywhere connection.

Scale

Networks are often classified as local area network (LAN), wide area network (WAN), metropolitan area network (MAN), personal area network (PAN), virtual private network (VPN), campus area network (CAN), storage area network (SAN), and others, depending on their scale, scope and purpose. (e.g., Controller Area Network (CAN)) Usage, trust level, and access right often differ between these types of network. For example, LANs tend to be designed for internal use by an organization's internal systems and employees in individual physical locations (such as a building), while WANs may connect physically separate parts of an organization and may include connections to third parties.

Functional Relationship (Network Architecture)

Computer networks may be classified according to the functional relationships which exist among the elements of the network, e.g., active networking, client–server and peer-to-peer (workgroup) architecture.

Computer Network

Computer networks may be classified according to the network topology upon which the network is based, such as bus network, star network, ring network, mesh network, star-bus network, tree or hierarchical topology network. Network topology is the coordination by which devices in the network are arranged in their logical relations to one another, independent of physical arrangement. Even if networked computers are physically placed in a linear arrangement and are connected to a hub, the network has a star topology, rather than a bus topology. In this regard the visual and operational characteristics of a network are distinct. Networks may be classified based on the method of data used to convey the data, these include digital and analog networks.

Types of Networks

Common types of computer networks may be identified by their scale.

Personal Area Network

A personal area network (PAN) is a computer network used for communication among computer and different information technological devices close to one person. Some examples of devices that are used in a PAN are personal computers, printers, fax machines, telephones, PDAs, scanners, and even video game consoles. A PAN may include wired and wireless connections between devices. The reach of a PAN typically extends to 10 meters. Wired PAN network is usually constructed with USB and Firewire while wireless with Bluetooth and Infrared.

Local Area Network

A local area network (LAN) is a network that connects computers and devices in a limited geographical area such as home, school, computer laboratory, office building, or closely positioned group of buildings. Each computer or device on the network is a node. Current wired LANs are most likely to be based on Ethernet technology, although new standards like ITU-T G.hn also provide a way to create a wired LAN using existing home wires (coaxial cables, phone lines and power lines).

Typical library network, in a branching tree topology and controlled access to resources.

All interconnected devices must understand the network layer (layer 3), because they are handling multiple subnets (the different colors). Those inside the library, which have only 10/100 Mbit/s Ethernet connections to the user device and a Gigabit Ethernet connection to the central router, could be called "layer 3 switches" because they only have Ethernet interfaces and must understand IP. It would be more correct to call them access routers, where the router at the top is a distribution router that connects to the Internet and academic networks' customer access routers.

The defining characteristics of LANs, in contrast to WANs (Wide Area Networks), include their higher data transfer rates, smaller geographic range, and no need for leased telecommunication lines. Current Ethernet or other IEEE 802.3 LAN technologies operate at speeds up to 10 Gbit/

s. This is the data transfer rate. IEEE has projects investigating the standardization of 40 and 100 Gbit/s.

Home Area Network

A home area network is a residential LAN which is used for communication between digital devices typically deployed in the home, usually a small number of personal computers and accessories, such as printers and mobile computing devices. An important function is the sharing of Internet access, often a broadband service through a CATV or Digital Subscriber Line (DSL) provider.

Campus Network

A campus network is a computer network made up of an interconnection of local area networks (LANs) within a limited geographical area. The networking equipments (switches, routers) and transmission media (optical fibre, copper plant, Cat5 cabling etc.) are almost entirely owned (by the campus tenant/owner: an enterprise, university, government etc.).

In the case of a university campus-based campus network, the network is likely to link a variety of campus buildings including; academic departments, the university library and student residence halls.

A network links two ore more computers together to communicate and share resources. Using your classroom notes, the Internet, magazines, or other resources, conduct a research about computer networks. Prepare a brief research paper (200-300 words) that discusses what a network is, what LAN, WAN, is and what the primary network components are. Include two references, one of which must be a Web site on the Internet.

Wide Area Network

A wide area network (WAN) is a computer network that covers a large geographic area such as a city, country, or spans even intercontinental distances, using a communications channel that combines many types of media such as telephone lines, cables, and air waves. A WAN often uses transmission facilities provided by common carriers, such as telephone companies. WAN technologies generally function at the lower three layers of the OSI reference model: the physical layer, the data link layer, and the network layer.

Global Area Network

A global area network (GAN) is a network used for supporting mobile communications across an arbitrary number of wireless LANs, satellite coverage areas, etc. The key challenge in mobile communications is handing off the user communications from one local coverage area to the next. In IEEE Project 802, this involves a succession of terrestrial WIRELESS local area networks (WLAN).

Enterprise Private Network

Sample EPN made of Frame relay WAN connections and dialup remote access.

Beginning with the digitalisation of telecommunication networks started in the 70's in the USA (by AT&T) and propelled by the growth in computer systems availability and demands private networks have been built for decades without the need to append the term private to them. The networks were operated over telecommunication networks and as per voice communications a certain amount of security and secrecy was expected and assumed.

But with the Internet in the 90's came a new type of network built over this Public infrastructure, using encryption to protect the data traffic from eaves-dropping (VPN). So the enterprise networks are now commonly referred to Enterprise Private Network in order to clarify that these are private networks (in opposition to public networks).

Virtual Private Network

Sample VPN used to interconnect 3 office and Remote users

A virtual private network (VPN) is a computer network in which some of the links between nodes are carried by open connections or virtual circuits in some larger network (e.g., the Internet) instead of by physical wires. The data link layer protocols of the virtual network are said to be tunneled through the larger network when this is the case. One common application is secure communications through the public Internet, but a VPN need not have explicit security features, such as authentication or content encryption. VPNs, for example, can be used to separate the traffic of different user communities over an underlying network with strong security features.

A VPN may have best-effort performance, or may have a defined service level agreement (SLA) between the VPN customer and the VPN service provider. Generally, a VPN has a topology more complex than point-to-point.

Internetwork

An Internetwork is the connection of two or more private computer networks via a common switching (OSI Layer 2) or routing technology (OSI Layer 3) and owned by separate entities (public or private). The result is called an internetwork. The Internet is an aggregation of many Internetworks hence it's name was shortened to Internet.

Any interconnection between public, private, commercial, industrial, or governmental networks may also be defined as an internetwork or (more often) an extranet.

Internet

The Internet is a global system of interconnected governmental, academic, corporate, public, and private computer networks. It is based on the networking technologies of the Internet Protocol Suite. It is the successor of the Advanced Research Projects Agency Network (ARPANET) developed by DARPA of the U.S. Department of Defense. The Internet is also the communications backbone underlying the World Wide Web (WWW). The 'Internet' is most commonly spelled with a capital 'I' as a proper noun, for historical reasons and to distinguish it from other generic internetworks.

Participants in the Internet use a diverse array of methods of several hundred documented, and often standardized, protocols compatible with the Internet Protocol Suite and an addressing system (IP Addresses) administered by the Internet Assigned Numbers Authority and address registries. Service providers and large enterprises exchange information about the reachability of their address spaces through the Border Gateway Protocol (BGP), forming a redundant worldwide mesh of transmission paths.

Intranets and Extranets

Intranets and extranets are parts or extensions of a computer network, usually a local area network.

An intranet is a set of networks, using the Internet Protocol and IP-based tools such as web browsers and file transfer applications, that is under the control of a single administrative entity. That administrative entity closes the intranet to all but specific, authorized users. Most commonly, an intranet is the internal network of an organization. A large intranet will typically have at least one web server to provide users with organizational information.

An extranet is a network that is limited in scope to a single organization or entity and also has limited connections to the networks of one or more other usually, but not necessarily, trusted organizations or entities (e.g., a company's customers may be given access to some part of its intranet creating in this way an extranet, while at the same time the customers may not be considered 'trusted' from a security standpoint). Technically, an extranet may also be categorized as a CAN, MAN, WAN, or other type of network, although, by definition, an extranet cannot consist of a single LAN; it must have at least one connection with an external network.

Overlay Network

An overlay network is a computer network that is built on top of another network. Nodes in the overlay can be thought of as being connected by virtual or logical links, each of which corresponds to a path, perhaps through many physical links, in the underlying network. For example, many peer-to-peer networks are overlay networks because they run on top of the Internet. Internet was built as an overlay upon the telephone network.

Overlay networks have been around since the invention of networking when computer systems were connected over telephone lines using modem, before any data network existed.

Nowadays the Internet is the basis for many overlaid networks than can be constructed in order to permit routing of messages to destinations not specified by an IP address. For example, distributed hash tables can be used to route messages to a node having a specific logical address, whose IP address is not known in advance.

Overlay networks have also been proposed as a way to improve Internet routing, such as through quality of service guarantees to achieve higher-quality streaming media. Previous proposals such as IntServ, DiffServ, and IP Multicast have not seen wide acceptance largely because they require modification of all routers in the network. On the other hand, an overlay network can be incrementally deployed on end-hosts running the overlay protocol software, without cooperation from ISPs. The overlay has no control over how packets are routed in the underlying network between two overlay nodes, but it can control, for example, the sequence of overlay nodes a message traverses before reaching its destination.

For example, Akamai Technologies manages an overlay network which provides reliable, efficient content delivery (a kind of multicast). Academic research includes End System Multicast and Overcast for multicast; RON (Resilient Overlay Network) for resilient routing; and OverQoS for quality of service guarantees, among others.

Basic Hardware Components

All networks are made up of basic hardware building blocks to interconnect network nodes, such as Network Interface Cards (NICs), Bridges, Hubs, Switches, and Routers. In addition, some methods of connecting these building blocks is required, usually in the form of galvanic cable (most commonly Category 5 cable). Less common are microwave links (as in IEEE 802.12) or optical cable ("optical fibre"). An Ethernet card may also be required.

Network Interface Cards

A network card, network adapter, or NIC (network interface card) is a piece of computer hardware designed to allow computers to communicate over a computer network. It provides physical access to a networking medium and often provides a low-level addressing system through the use of MAC addresses.

Repeaters

A repeater is an electronic device that receives a signal, cleans it from the unnecessary noise, regenerates it and retransmits it at a higher power level, or to the other side of an obstruction, so that the signal can cover longer distances without degradation. In most twisted pair Ethernet configurations, repeaters are required for cable which runs longer than 100 meters. Repeaters work on the Physical Layer of the OSI model.

Hubs

A network hub contains multiple ports. When a packet arrives at one port, it is copied unmodified to all ports of the hub for transmission. The destination address in the frame is not changed to a broadcast address. It works on the Physical Layer of the OSI model.

Bridges

A network bridge connects multiple network segments at the data link layer (layer 2) of the OSI model. Bridges do send broadcasts to all ports except the one on which the broadcast was received. However, bridges do not promiscuously copy traffic to all ports, as hubs do, but learn which MAC addresses are reachable through specific ports. Once the bridge associates a port and an address, it will send traffic for that address to that port only.

Bridges learn the association of ports and addresses by examining the source address of frames that it sees on various ports. Once a frame arrives through a port, its source address is stored and the bridge assumes that MAC address is associated with that port. The first time that a previously unknown destination address is seen, the bridge will forward the frame to all ports other than the one on which the frame arrived.

Bridges come in three basic types:

- Local bridges: Directly connect local area networks (LANs)
- Remote bridges: Can be used to create a wide area network (WAN) link between LANs. Remote bridges, where the connecting link is slower than the end networks, largely have been replaced with routers.
- Wireless bridges: Can be used to join LANs or connect remote stations to LANs

Switches

A network switch is a device that forwards and filters OSI layer 2 datagrams (chunk of data communication) between ports (connected cables) based on the MAC addresses in the packets. This is distinct from a hub in that it only forwards the frames to the ports involved in the communication rather than all ports connected. A switch breaks the collision domain but represents itself a broadcast domain. Switches make forwarding decisions of frames on the basis of MAC addresses. A switch normally has numerous ports, facilitating a star topology for devices, and cascading additional switches. Some switches are capable of routing based on Layer 3 addressing or additional logical levels; these are called multi-layer switches. The term *switch* is used loosely in marketing to encompass devices including routers and bridges, as well as devices that may distribute traffic on load or by application content (e.g., a Web URL identifier).

Routers

A router is a networking device that forwards packets between networks using information in protocol headers and forwarding tables to determine the best next router for each packet.

Network Topology

In computer networking, topology refers to the layout of connected devices.

Network topology is defined as the physical interconnection of the various elements (links, nodes, etc.) of a computer network. Network Topologies can be physical or logical. Physical Topology means the physical design of a network including the devices, location and cable installation. Logical topology refers to the fact that how data actually transfers in a network as opposed to its design.

Topology can be considered as a virtual shape or structure of a network. This shape actually does not correspond to the actual physical design of the devices on the computer network. The computers on the home network can be arranged in a circle shape but it does not necessarily mean that it presents a ring topology.

Any particular network topology is determined only by the graphical mapping of the configuration of physical and/ or logical connections between nodes. The study of network topology uses graph theory. Distances between nodes, physical interconnections, transmission rates, and/or signal types may differ in two networks and yet their topologies may be identical.

A Local Area Network (LAN) is one example of a network that exhibits both a physical topology and a logical topology. Any given node in the LAN has one or more links to one or more nodes in the network and the mapping of these links and nodes in a graph results in a geometrical shape that may be used to describe the physical topology of the network. Likewise, the mapping of the data flow between the nodes in the network determines the logical topology of the network. The physical and logical topologies may or may not be identical in any particular network.

Basic Topology Types

The study of network topology recognizes four basic topologies:

- Bus topology
- Star topology
- Ring topology
- Tree topology

This classification is based on the interconnection between computers—be it physical or logical.

Classification of Network Topologies

There are also three basic categories of network topologies:

- Physical topologies
- Signal topologies
- Logical topologies

The terms Signal topology and logical topology are often used interchangeably, though there is a subtle difference between the two.

Physical Topologies

The mapping of the nodes of a network and the physical connections between them – i.e., the layout of wiring, cables, the locations of nodes, and the interconnections between the nodes and the cabling or wiring system.

Classification of Physical Topologies

Point-to-point: The simplest topology is a permanent link between two endpoints (the line in the illustration above). Switched point-to-point topologies are the basic model of conventional telephony. The value of a permanent point-to-point network is the value of guaranteed, or nearly so, communications between the two endpoints. The value of an on-demand point-to-point connection is proportional to the number of potential pairs of subscribers, and has been expressed as Metcalfe's Law.

Permanent (dedicated): Easiest to understand, of the variations of point-to-point topology, is a point-to-point communications channel that appears, to the user, to be permanently associated with the two endpoints. Children's "tin-can telephone" is one example, with a microphone to a single public address speaker is another. These are examples of *physical dedicated* channels.

Within many switched telecommunications systems, it is possible to establish a permanent circuit. One example might be a telephone in the lobby of a public building, which is programmed to ring only the number of a telephone dispatcher. "Nailing down" a switched connection saves the cost of running a physical circuit between the two points.

The resources in such a connection can be released when no longer needed, for example, a television circuit from a parade route back to the studio.

Switched: Using circuit-switching or packet-switching technologies, a point-to-point circuit can be set-up dynamically, and dropped when no longer needed. This is the basic mode of conventional telephony.

Bus

Bus Network Topology: In local area networks where bus topology is used, each machine is connected to a single cable. Each computer or server is connected to the single bus cable through some kind of connector. A terminator is required at each end of the bus cable to prevent the signal from bouncing back and forth on the bus cable. A signal from the source travels in both directions to all machines connected on the bus cable until it finds the MAC address or IP address on the network that is the intended recipient. If the machine address does not match the intended address for the data, the machine ignores the data. Alternatively, if the data does match the machine address, the data is accepted. Since the bus topology consists of only one wire, it is rather inexpensive to implement when compared to other topologies. However, the low cost of implementing the technology is offset by the high cost of managing the network. Additionally, since only one cable is utilized, it can be the single point of failure. If the network cable breaks, the entire network will be down.

Linear Bus: The type of network topology in which all of the nodes of the network are connected to a common transmission medium which has exactly two endpoints (this is the 'bus', which is also commonly referred to as the backbone, or trunk) – all data that is transmitted between nodes in the network is transmitted over this common transmission medium and is able to be received by all nodes in the network virtually simultaneously (disregarding propagation delays).

Note: The two endpoints of the common transmission medium are normally terminated with a device called a terminator that exhibits the characteristic impedance of the transmission medium and which dissipates or absorbs the energy that remains in the signal to prevent the signal from being reflected or propagated back onto the transmission medium in the opposite direction, which would cause interference with and degradation of the signals on the transmission medium.

Distributed Bus: The type of network topology in which all of the nodes of the network are connected to a common transmission medium which has more than two endpoints that are created by adding branches to the main section of the transmission medium – the physical distributed bus topology functions in exactly the same fashion as the physical linear bus topology (i.e., all nodes share a common transmission medium).

Notes:

(1) All of the endpoints of the common transmission medium are normally terminated with a device called a 'terminator'.

(2) The physical linear bus topology is sometimes considered to be a special case of the physical distributed bus topology i.e., a distributed bus with no branching segments.

(3) The physical distributed bus topology is sometimes incorrectly referred to as a physical tree topology however, although the physical distributed bus topology resembles the physical tree topology, it differs from the physical tree topology in that there is no central node to which any other nodes are connected, since this hierarchical functionality is replaced by the common bus.

Star

Star network topology: In local area networks with a star topology, each network host is connected to a central hub. In contrast to the bus topology, the star topology connects each node to the hub with a point-to-point connection. All traffic that transverses the network passes through the central hub. The hub acts as a signal booster or repeater. The star topology is considered the easiest topology to design and implement. An advantage of the star topology is the simplicity of adding additional nodes. The primary disadvantage of the star topology is that the hub represents a single point of failure.

Notes:

- A point-to-point link (described above) is sometimes categorized as a special instance of the physical star topology therefore, the simplest type of network that is based upon the physical star topology would consist of one node with a single point-to-point link to a second node, the choice of which node is the 'hub' and which node is the 'spoke' being arbitrary.
- After the special case of the point-to-point link, as in note 1.) above, the next simplest type of network that is based upon the physical star topology would consist of one central node the 'hub' with two separate point-to-point links to two peripheral nodes the 'spokes'.
- Although most networks that are based upon the physical star topology are commonly implemented using a special device such as a hub or switch as the central node (i.e., the 'hub' of the star), it is also possible to implement a network that is based upon the physical star topology using a computer or even a simple common connection point as the 'hub' or central node however, since many illustrations of the physical star network topology depict the central node as one of these special devices, some confusion is possible, since this practice may lead to the misconception that a physical star network requires the central node to be one of these special devices, which is not true because a simple network

consisting of three computers connected as in notes 2.) above also has the topology of the physical star.

- Star networks may also be described as either broadcast multi-access or nonbroadcast multi-access (NBMA), depending on whether the technology of the network either automatically propagates a signal at the hub to all spokes, or only addresses individual spokes with each communication.

Extended Star: A type of network topology in which a network that is based upon the physical star topology has one or more repeaters between the central node (the 'hub' of the star) and the peripheral or 'spoke' nodes, the repeaters being used to extend the maximum transmission distance of the point-to-point links between the central node and the peripheral nodes beyond that which is supported by the transmitter power of the central node or beyond that which is supported by the standard upon which the physical layer of the physical star network is based.

If the repeaters in a network that is based upon the physical extended star topology are replaced with hubs or switches, then a hybrid network topology is created that is referred to as a physical hierarchical star topology, although some texts make no distinction between the two topologies.

Distributed Star: A type of network topology that is composed of individual networks that are based upon the physical star topology connected together in a linear fashion – i.e., 'daisy-chained' – with no central or top level connection point (e.g., two or more 'stacked' hubs, along with their associated star connected nodes or 'spokes').

Ring

Ring network topology: In local area networks where the ring topology is used, each computer is connected to the network in a closed loop or ring. Each machine or computer has a unique address that is used for identification purposes. The signal passes through each machine or computer connected to the ring in one direction. Ring topologies typically utilize a token passing scheme, used to control access to the network. By utilizing this scheme, only one machine can transmit on the network at a time. The machines or computers connected to the ring act as signal boosters or repeaters which strengthen the signals that transverse the network. The primary disadvantage of ring topology is the failure of one machine will cause the entire network to fail.

Mesh

The value of fully meshed networks is proportional to the exponent of the number of subscribers, assuming that communicating groups of any two endpoints, up to and including all the endpoints, is approximated by Reed's Law.

Fully Connected Mesh Topology

Fully connected

Note: The physical fully connected mesh topology is generally too costly and complex for practical networks, although the topology is used when there are only a small number of nodes to be interconnected.

Partially Connected Mesh Topology

Partially connected

The type of network topology in which some of the nodes of the network are connected to more than one other node in the network with a point-to-point link this makes it possible to take advantage of some of the redundancy that is provided by a physical fully connected mesh topology without the expense and complexity required for a connection between every node in the network.

Note: In most practical networks that are based upon the physical partially connected mesh topology, all of the data that is transmitted between nodes in the network takes the shortest path (or an approximation of the shortest path) between nodes, except in the case of a failure or break in one of the links, in which case the data takes an alternative path to the destination. This requires that the nodes of the network possess some type of logical 'routing' algorithm to determine the correct path to use at any particular time.

Tree

Tree network topology: Also known as a hierarchical network.

The type of network topology in which a central 'root' node (the top level of the hierarchy) is connected to one or more other nodes that are one level lower in the hierarchy (i.e., the second level) with a point-to-point link between each of the second level nodes and the top level central 'root' node, while each of the second level nodes that are connected to the top level central 'root' node will also have one or more other nodes that are one level lower in the hierarchy (i.e., the third level) connected to it, also with a point-to-point link, the top level central 'root' node being the only node that has no other node above it in the hierarchy (The hierarchy of the tree is symmetrical.) Each node in the network having a specific fixed number, of nodes connected to it at the next lower level in the hierarchy, the number, being referred to as the 'branching factor' of the hierarchical tree.

(1) A network that is based upon the physical hierarchical topology must have at least three levels in the hierarchy of the tree, since a network with a central 'root' node and only one hierarchical level below it would exhibit the physical topology of a star.

(2) A network that is based upon the physical hierarchical topology and with a branching factor of 1 would be classified as a physical linear topology.

(3) The branching factor, f, is independent of the total number of nodes in the network and, therefore, if the nodes in the network require ports for connection to other nodes the total number of ports per node may be kept low even though the total number of

nodes is large this makes the effect of the cost of adding ports to each node totally dependent upon the branching factor and may therefore be kept as low as required without any effect upon the total number of nodes that are possible.

(4) The total number of point-to-point links in a network that is based upon the physical hierarchical topology will be one less than the total number of nodes in the network.

(5) If the nodes in a network that is based upon the physical hierarchical topology are required to perform any processing upon the data that is transmitted between nodes in the network, the nodes that are at higher levels in the hierarchy will be required to perform more processing operations on behalf of other nodes than the nodes that are lower in the hierarchy. Such a type of network topology is very useful and highly recommended.

Signal Topology

The mapping of the actual connections between the nodes of a network, as evidenced by the path that the signals take when propagating between the nodes.

Note: The term 'signal topology' is often used synonymously with the term 'logical topology', however, some confusion may result from this practice in certain situations since, by definition, the term 'logical topology' refers to the apparent path that the data takes between nodes in a network while the term 'signal topology' generally refers to the actual path that the signals (e.g., optical, electrical, electromagnetic, etc.) take when propagating between nodes.

Logical Topology

The logical topology, in contrast to the "physical", is the way that the signals act on the network media, or the way that the data passes through the network from one device to the next without regard to the physical interconnection of the devices. A network's logical topology is not necessarily the same as its physical topology. For example, twisted pair Ethernet is a logical bus topology in a physical star topology layout. While IBM's Token Ring is a logical ring topology, it is physically set up in a star topology.

Classification of Logical Topologies

The logical classification of network topologies generally follows the same classifications as those in the physical classifications of network topologies, the path that the *data* takes between nodes being used to determine the topology as opposed to the actual *physical* connections being used to determine the gyutt.

Notes:

(1) Logical topologies are often closely associated with media access control (MAC) methods and protocols.

(2) The logical topologies are generally determined by network protocols as opposed to being determined by the physical layout of cables, wires, and network devices or by the flow of the electrical signals, although in many cases the paths that the electrical signals take between nodes may closely match the logical flow of data, hence the convention of using the terms 'logical topology' and 'signal topology' interchangeably.

(3) Logical topologies are able to be dynamically reconfigured by special types of equipment such as routers and switches.

Daisy Chains

Except for star-based networks, the easiest way to add more computers into a network is by daisy-chaining, or connecting each computer in series to the next. If a message is intended for a computer partway down the line, each system bounces it along in sequence until it reaches the destination. A daisy-chained network can take two basic forms: linear and ring.

- A linear topology puts a two-way link between one computer and the next. However, this was expensive in the early days of computing, since each computer (except for the ones at each end) required two receivers and two transmitters.
- By connecting the computers at each end, a ring topology can be formed. An advantage of the ring is that the number of transmitters and receivers can be cut in half, since a message will eventually loop all of the way around. When a node sends a message, the message is processed by each computer in the ring. If a computer is not the destination node, it will pass the message to the next node, until the message arrives at its destination. If the message is not accepted by any node on the network, it will travel around the entire ring and return to the sender. This potentially results in a doubling of travel time for data.

Centralization

The star topology reduces the probability of a network failure by connecting all of the peripheral nodes (computers, etc.) to a central node. When the physical star topology is applied to a logical bus network such as Ethernet, this central node (traditionally a hub) rebroadcasts all transmissions received from any peripheral node to all peripheral nodes on the network, sometimes including the originating node. All peripheral nodes may thus communicate with all others by transmitting to, and receiving from, the central node only. The failure of a transmission line linking any peripheral node to the central node will result in the isolation of that peripheral node from all others, but the remaining peripheral nodes will be unaffected. However, the disadvantage is that the failure of the central node will cause the failure of all of the peripheral nodes also.

If the central node is *passive*, the originating node must be able to tolerate the reception of an echo of its own transmission, delayed by the two-way round trip transmission time (i.e. to and from the central node) plus any delay generated in the central node. An *active* star network has an active central node that usually has the means to prevent echo-related problems.

A tree topology (a.k.a. hierarchical topology) can be viewed as a collection of star networks arranged in a hierarchy. This tree has individual peripheral nodes (e.g. leaves) which are required to transmit to and receive from one other node only and are not required to act as repeaters or regenerators. Unlike the star network, the functionality of the central node may be distributed.

As in the conventional star network, individual nodes may thus still be isolated from the network by a single-point failure of a transmission path to the node. If a link connecting a leaf fails, that leaf is isolated; if a connection to a non-leaf node fails, an entire section of the network becomes isolated from the rest.

In order to alleviate the amount of network traffic that comes from broadcasting all signals to all nodes, more advanced central nodes were developed that are able to keep track of the identities of the nodes that are connected to the network. These network switches will "learn" the layout of the network by "listening" on each port during normal data transmission, examining the data packets and recording the address/identifier of each connected node and which port it's connected to in a lookup table held in memory. This lookup table then allows future transmissions to be forwarded to the intended destination only.

Decentralization

In a mesh topology (i.e., a partially connected mesh topology), there are at least two nodes with two or more paths between them to provide redundant paths to be used in case the link providing one of the paths fails. This decentralization is often used to advantage to compensate for the single-point-failure disadvantage that is present when using a single device as a central node (e.g., in star and tree networks). A special kind of mesh, limiting the number of hops between two nodes, is a hypercube. The number of arbitrary forks in mesh networks makes them more difficult to design and implement, but their decentralized nature makes them very useful. This is similar in some ways to a grid network, where a linear or ring topology is used to connect systems in multiple directions. A multi-dimensional ring has a toroidal topology, for instance.

A fully connected network, complete topology or full mesh topology is a network topology in which there is a direct link between all pairs of nodes. In a fully connected network with n nodes, there are $n(n-1)/2$ direct links. Networks designed with this topology are usually very expensive to set up, but provide a high degree of reliability due to the multiple paths for data that are provided by the large number of redundant links between nodes. This topology is mostly seen in military applications. However, it can also be seen in the file sharing protocol BitTorrent in which users connect to other users in the "swarm" by allowing each user sharing the file to connect to other users also involved. Often in actual usage of BitTorrent any given individual node is rarely connected to every single other node as in a true fully connected network but the protocol does allow for the possibility for any one node to connect to any other node when sharing files.

Hybrids

Hybrid networks use a combination of any two or more topologies in such a way that the resulting network does not exhibit one of the standard topologies (e.g., bus, star, ring, etc.). For example, a tree network connected to a tree network is still a tree network, but two star networks connected together exhibit a hybrid network topology. A hybrid topology is always produced when two different basic network topologies are connected. Two common examples for Hybrid network are: *star ring network* and *star bus network:*

- A Star Ring network consists of two or more star topologies connected using a multistation access unit (MAU) as a centralized hub.
- A Star Bus network consists of two or more star topologies connected using a bus trunk (the bus trunk serves as the network's backbone).

While grid networks have found popularity in high-performance computing applications, some systems have used genetic algorithms to design custom networks that have the fewest possible hops in between different nodes. Some of the resulting layouts are nearly incomprehensible, although they function quite well.

6

Education in Information Society and Computer Age

Introduction

Education was one of the few sectors which remained relatively stable during the early decades of the all-pervasive ICT-based revolution which has been charted throughout this book. In the 1990s, however, education began to face the full brunt of a global maelstrom driven by ICT. This was because education held a near-monopoly on the important middle ground separating work and play in most advanced economies.

The way in which communications can change old ways by closing the gap between work and play was first demonstrated by the growth of teleworking in the 1990s. This kind of change makes the very concept of a distinct education sector become increasingly tenuous as community and customer requirements undermine traditional frameworks and institutions. Organizations designed to cope with stable environments and limited information flows find it increasingly difficult to cope as they move towards a new environment. In this, information, education, training, expertise, and ultimately, experience are expected to be delivered on demand at the time and place they are wanted—Just-In-Time (JIT), to use the phrase coined in the manufacturing industry. The assumptions on which such organizations were based in the past therefore no longer 'fit reality'.

Turbulence in the global economy, in which ICT plays a key role, is thus likely to trigger the absorption of much of the education sector into a new 'experience industry'. This will encompass sectors like entertainment and tourism and rely extensively on a variety of telecommunications-based 'tele-services' and the application of virtual reality capabilities. Such developments present immense opportunities for co-operative forms of global wealth creation.

They also mean many enterprises are having to adopt new organizational forms which must be resilient and able to adjust to new environments continually as all institutions have to become increasingly fluid, agile, and obsessively customer-facing in order to maintain direction and survive in intensely competitive markets. The growing uncertainties and shortening timescales in this global economy are challenging centralized organizations and structures in all their varied forms political, economic, social, managerial, and technological. Centralized control and management can no longer handle the vast and increasingly rapid information flows involved while at the same time allowing reflexive local decision making processes.

Turbulence in the global marketplace will continue apace as newer developing economies become comparable with North America, Western Europe, and other developed regions. The resulting escalation in the mobility of economic and technological activity across international borders will see bleak prospects for traditional industries and their old working practices. New flexible forms of industry are needed to succeed in the emerging 'super-advanced economies' operating at even higher speed than in the latter part of the twentieth century.

Telecommunications and Competition

The super-advanced economy will rely, initially at least, on a synthesis of manufacturing and servicing capabilities for 'tele-exporting' within global markets, as well as a variety of other new economic activities. The intensification of competition and rapid wealth redistribution will then become a day-by-day norm. In the transition, unstable enterprises will 'melt down' when their traditional organizational manifestations disappear. However, the people, money, and resources will metamorphose into many smaller organizations. The telecommunications industry was one of the first to do this when public telephone utilities with established national monopolies were transformed into large numbers of small, highly competitive, customer-oriented units.

The waves of meltdown will grow as digital technologies converge and competitors rush into overlapping new markets. The future of the global economy depends fundamentally on the ability to use advanced ICT capabilities to transfer and process vast amounts of information across geographical borders, markets and organizations. It is no longer possible to operate in isolation when communications across organizational and geographical boundaries become so easy and efficient. As a result, many 'virtualizing' services become feasible. For example, on-demand interaction at a distance can be mediated through 'telepresence' capabilities which allow users to experience multimedia information, communication, and processing as if they were 'real' entities. Telepresence further stimulates creativity, allows choice to multiply, and underpins advanced co-operative global wealth creation—while the inherent ability of telecommunications to act as a conduit increases with the growing capacity to combine different media.

The ICT revolution started in the factory and office, then entered the home in the form of integrated entertainment and information systems. As advances in chip, satellite, radio, and optical-fibre technologies further reach out to the car and individual, distinctions between work, education, and play dissolve. The way business is conducted, economies are driven, and education is delivered will change dramatically as more people are able to choose where, and with whom, they carry out these activities. 'Virtual teams' can be located around the globe while working together through networked interactions. Programmes, projects, developments, creativity, and collaboration can then be non-stop and transnational, with rapid responses and very high productivity.

Transforming Education

Education is typical of those sectors likely to be caught in the second wave of meltdowns prompted by the increasing availability of communication and information capabilities. ICTs remove the constraints of distance, time, and location, which will undermine traditional educational monopolies and force a restructuring and revitalization as a new 'training, learning, and creativity' sector. In common with other industries, a hybrid of innovations both within and outside the sector will be needed to sustain growth through the global transition.

'Micro-hybridization' of detailed educational activities is evidenced by the widespread introduction of modular courses which allow the integration of previously separate subjects to meet specific industry, business, and lifestyle needs. In many technology areas, university degrees can become outdated within a few years. Lifetime learning has become a necessity and will replace the old pattern in which education occurred in school and university before a person started a career. Meltdown in education is also likely to encompass all ages and bring remote capabilities into the home.

These developments are pushing education into extensive 'macrohybridization', such as in the moving closer together of previously distinct education and entertainment activities to spawn an 'edutainment' sector fuelled by new consumer electronic products. Even traditionally stable domains such as mathematics and the classics are being radically changed through visualization, modelling, and animation techniques created to excite the individual learner.

Online self-learning packages fundamentally question the traditional role of the educator by giving students greater individual control. Effective learning can be realized by providing a student with a computer, loading the educational software, and walking away. As this becomes a natural teaching environment for younger people, it may be necessary to use only traditional methods with 'older' students.

Integrating the Learning Structure

New forms of economic activity must offer competitive advantages over those already established. If they do not, the hyper connected global market will react quickly and bypass them. The requirement for new forms of activity indicates that advanced economies must invest new learning skills in their people. A super-advanced economy will work only if it is super creative, with the ability to market and sell its creations rapidly. Economic activity relying on the deployment of unskilled labour is extremely unlikely to form the basis of healthy and sustainable social structures.

Unskilled, low-cost, low-value-added labour markets will be decimated, perhaps leading to the formation of economic and knowledge ghettos locked out from global participation and society. There is, therefore, a real prospect of the formation of a permanent underclass. The overriding requirement is for rapid and high-density learning, education, and training in support of the new rapid-creativity industries, many of which may be in, or very close to, the home. Hence education and training must be transformed into all-pervasive, boundary crossing learning and creativity activities.

Many of the newly emerging economies have exceptionally young and massive populations, reinforcing the vital need for super-advanced economies to develop and tap the skills of every citizen. Future economies cannot afford the learning and creativity sector to be separate from the rest of society. It must permeate every aspect of society and embrace all of the people. Everyone must be given the opportunity to contribute.

Education Monopolies

In most industrialized countries education has evolved to become a monopoly employing relatively slow processes. These monopolies have been challenged by a global economic and technological turbulence. In addition, there is a substantial growth in the creation of advanced knowledge and innovation outside education in the 'knowledge businesses'. The education sector is thus losing its monopoly on knowledge creation. In the UK, for example, all the university research programs in the mid-1980s were totally overshadowed and largely outclassed by the industrial sector, with some companies investing more in R&D than government-sponsored Research Councils. The ratio of industrial to university expenditure and achievement is even greater in Japan, the USA, and some other European countries. Nevertheless, universities remain a vital and vibrant part of the system, although they provide only a small percentage of the total research activity.

Education is unable to contribute meaningfully in areas whose levels of investment necessary in the more sophisticated technological areas are too great. R&D can thus become rapidly denuded as companies seek relevant expertise and innovations beyond their national boundaries. In this situation, the involvement of all levels of industry in academic programs are important, offering benefits to both sides. Academia brings a freshness that can be quite powerful, while industry exposes academics to the complex world of commercial R&D and operations. For example, it should be possible for students to link into industry through projects which present meaningful challenges at all levels. Work programs should be farmed out as undergraduate and postgraduate projects, with sponsored R&D supporting researchers in industry and universities.

Knowledge businesses, with their life-long learners, have an important advantage over traditional educational institutions because their operating environment compels them to develop forward-looking and responsive capabilities. Knowledge businesses should see themselves and their customers in partnerships, with both partners playing the role of educator and learner. The synergistic relationship of education, training, knowledge, and business has become essential for their mutual survival and prosperity. The transformation of education and training will bring numerous opportunities to those active in building the new flexible learning and creativity structures. It will also provide new choices for the millions of new global customers waiting to be offered new telelearning experiences.

Virtualizing Education

Developments in multimedia, increased communication, and other ICT innovations are obviously key components of the information society. In this new era, managers must be prepared to abandon everything they know and the same may hold for teachers, educationalists, researchers, students, and policy makers. Maintaining the status quo is not an option.

Numerous corporations and businesses have already become defunct or moribund through their adherence to the old markets and practices that made them. In contrast, other corporations are rapidly changing in structure and function as extended enterprises and virtual organizations emerge. These virtual organizations are not defined by physical space, but collaborative international networks linking people through integrated ICTs. For instance, the Integrated Digital Services Network (ISDN) available in many countries enables new modes of learning, working, and operation across a broad range of activities. These capabilities could make the 'virtual organization' the dominant organizational form, which is more about self-organization and emergent behaviour than planning and prediction. The advantages of moving to such a virtual approach based on tele-education and numerous novel partnerships to support training are key influences in transforming the education sector.

Technology developments needed to support such innovations can only be financed by diverting some of the enormous funds traditionally spent on activities such as physical travel, health, ICTs, and entertainment. Of these, physical travel is perhaps the least necessary, given its high cost in terms of raw material, energy, pollution, and time. Much of this could be avoided and largely replaced by ICT. Diverting into telecommunications-based activities even a modest percentage of this travel expenditure would enable considerable waste to be avoided through tele-activities.

Revolutionizing Education

To appreciate the challenges and opportunities facing education, it is instructive to examine the specific case of education in engineering. This is one of the fastest-moving industrial sectors and has been a leader in promoting technological, managerial, and operational change. The accelerating pace of technological innovation requires engineering education to be more responsive to industry and society, while also becoming more cost-effective. However, a key problem in many countries has been the lack of critical mass, which has resulted in university departments having insufficient staff to specialize and treat topics in sufficient depth, keep up-to-date, supervise research students, and develop new courses and teaching material. Moreover, it is clear that the pressures will not recede. It is, therefore, inevitable and essential that more productive forms of educational resourcing are realized.

The best teachers are able to put themselves in the student's place and impart their own insight in a graphic and enthusiastic way. With the acceleration of technological development and subsequent broadening of all curricula, the professionals who are successful in this process are becoming all too rare across the breadth of education. This has been overcome to some extent in the 'hard' sciences and technologies by, for example, using mathematical and physical models combined with 'handson' experience which rapidly facilitates understanding. The process is far more difficult in other subjects, especially the 'soft' human and social sciences, where students face a bewildering and expanding complexity. At the same time, financial budgets are constrained, as are course durations and schedules. All this promotes the need for the quick fix and rapid turnaround, combined with pressures to become more efficient, as in other sectors of the economy. Perhaps the key issue is whether education is becoming more effective as a result.

Due to various factors, it is unlikely that departments with the necessary critical mass will be realized simply through the co-location or coalescing of existing smaller units. The danger is that the global economy is fast unleashing forces which will destroy departments, colleges, and universities in their present form. With staff numbers and funding pared to the bone, there is no visible fat. This makes the education system increasingly vulnerable. Nevertheless, there is an alternative approach to achieving order-of-magnitude improvements in the efficiency of resource utilization and the stimulation of new forms of creativity. ICT can bring students and teachers together for lectures, tutorials, and one-to-one interactions across geographic locations. Many experiments can be conducted on the screen, while visualization techniques can greatly aid understanding through simulation and modelling. Such an approach could revolutionize teaching, training, learning, and research.

Multimedia Enhances Education

There are many thousands of libraries and information sources accessible online. CDs also provide vast stores of information, such as single discs containing thousands of works of classical literatures including the complete works of William Shakespeare or comprehensive encyclopedias. Interactive CDs can also allow students to 'visit' virtual museums, zoos, and landscapes so that they can make their own video-diaries of what they see. Such electronic capabilities continue to expand inexorably.

Compare this with the traditional world of paper. The US Library of Congress, for example, had about 24 million books in the mid-1990s and added new volumes which take about a further 3.5 km of shelving space each year. Libraries based on trying to keep pace with such volume and growth cannot be sustained. In most libraries, information is out of date, outmoded, disorganized, and irretrievable. The costs of physical searches are in themselves a major constraint, even if the existence of the required books or documents can be established. Online electronic libraries and CDs, on the other hand, can do all that much more quickly, at lower cost.

The most useful feature of a paper-based library, museum, or gallery is serendipity the chance happening upon something you were not looking for and the fortuitous cross-correlation of thoughts and ideas. Electronic libraries are capable of achieving similar benefits. As computer and other display screens grow larger, for example, it also becomes possible to view multiple documents and pages simultaneously. The libraries of old are thus to be eclipsed as the traditional paradigm of the printed page is expanded into a virtual 'hyperspace' in which documents have multiple layers of detail, extensive and flexible cross-linking, and great adaptability. Multimedia significantly added video, sound, animation, modelling, and interactivity while the technologies of telepresence and virtual reality introduce the richness needed to move from a world of information to an 'experience world'.

Since the Industrial Revolution, education has moved through all three lines of an old Chinese proverb:

> I hear and I forget
>
> I see and I remember
>
> I do and I understand.

We started with words, then included pictures, and finally experiments-as in university lecture theatres which traditionally have a demonstration bench right up front. Not so long ago, lectures and classes were commonly supported by physical demonstrations and 'hands on' sessions. Sadly, that has become increasingly rare, thereby diminishing the effectiveness of much teaching. The reasons for this backward step can be found in the exponentially growing curriculum, the tightening economy, the fixed education timeframe, and static mindsets. Salvation lies with the technology itself ICT allows a wide range of experiments to be on the screen. From the 1990s, many degree courses around the world have used the personal computer (PC) as a primary tool. To attend without access to a PC would be the equivalent of not having a pen or paper in earlier times.

Broadening Horizons

As the concept of using telecommunications to assist in education and training is increasingly accepted, environments incorporating dictums like 'you must have a PC to do a degree' and 'you must have PC skills to do the job' become intrinsic to more people's lives.

These transitions represent significant improvements over traditional methods in the utilization of educational resources, as well as indirectly assisting industrial competitiveness. In many cases, optimum benefits for individuals, groups, and communities will come from finding the most effective balance between these newer approaches and more traditional methods.

Virtual Universities for Real

Distance learning through ICT has been increasingly practical since the early 1990s, when successful experimental systems were established in many countries. This included the Open University in the UK, which in the 1960s pioneered the use of television for enabling mature students to get degrees. It conducted its first summer school over the Internet in 1994. In early 1993, the Robert Gordon University in Scotland conducted night-school classes over the telephone by broadcasting to over 250 students. In 1995, Stanford University in California launched its first online postgraduate degree course.

The distributed university clearly increases overall efficiency by teleporting students, teachers, and 'experience explorers' to virtual lecture theatres and environments. The notion that many students need to meet at the same physical place at the same time to watch one overworked teacher copy material from a book onto a blackboard, then allow it to

New Educational Opportunities Opened by Advanced ICTs

Lecturing and teaching do not necessarily have to take place in real-time.

Interactive multimedia databases and lectures could be accessed around the clock from the virtual electronic classroom.

Lecturers in numerous colleges and universities need no longer deliver substantially the same material. Instead, students and staff can be 'teleported' through telecommunications networks to common work spaces where they can interact. This releases valuable time which educators can use for activities such as research, consultancy, and generating new knowledge, understanding, and revenues.

Students will not have to be constrained to one university. They will haveu access to hundreds of different specialists, units, and centres across national borders and will be able to select the best and most inspirational teachers.

Students 'customers' can choose to build individualized courses engineered to suit their own lives, companies, and development. This could undermine national curricula.

Education and training can become a major export business by teleporting educational experiences to other countries.

Educational establishments can reduce investments in new buildings and halls of residence when their customer bases are extended globally, enabling state-of-the-art laboratories and libraries to be programmed, accessed, and shared in a virtual environment.

School, college, training course, and university 'opening hours' can be extended to 24 hours, seven days a week through virtual enterprises offering simulation technologies, teaching aids, and computer-based self-assessment.

Unhelpful distinctions between arts and sciences can be dissolved through the use of synthetic ICT-based environments which integrate teaching and research in disciplines such as choreography, acoustics, dynamics, and theatre design.

Students in 'virtual universities' can also work as company associates who contribute to designing and constructing real systems and products, as part of a synthesized process of training, learning, and experience acquisition.

Students are also likely to fare better if they are treated to individual expert lectures by specialists in each topic, combined with backup from local or remote tutors, mentors, counsellors, and guides.

As part of the growing demand for perpetual learning, there is also an increasing requirement in industry for online first and higher degrees, refresher courses, and higher levels of 'instant' understanding, Company staff are often too busy to spare time to travel to a college or university. Distance learning allows them to mix and match lectures and tutorials to create a learning portfolio of their choice, at times that fit with their other commitments.

For example, BT started to implement this concept in 1991 in the form of a 'distributed university' which offered Master's Degrees via interactive lectures using Integrated Digital Services Network (ISDN) services, with students gathered together physically in common locations to access each class. In 1995 BT opened the first virtual university, which enables teams of students in different locations to use the ISDN for interactive classes and tutorials. Students generally find this helps them to learn quickly, explore new areas without limiting subject demarcations, and, perhaps most important, develop their team working capabilities. Classes, lectures, tutorials, and experiments for this virtual university are presented and prepared by many universities and industrial organizations around the world, selected because they are regarded as the best of the best not just because they are close by and convenient.

As the global market becomes more competitive, the ability of organizations to bring teams together to tackle new problems for their customers will become crucial to survival. Business problems will come to resemble research problems as enterprises and their customers accelerate into the unknown. The ability to tap into virtual educational, learning, and training resources is thus a key strategic element. The virtual university, college, and school will be the hub by which learning organizations will begin to buzz with 'can-doism'.

Adding Substance to Virtualization

Simulation software and multimedia products offer animation, 'interactive theatre', and other capabilities which can help students understand and analyse complex issues. Experimentation and interaction with simulations on the screen also reduce the need for expensive physical laboratories. In addition, Artificial Intelligence (AI) techniques can be used to build systems that provide built-in expertise and knowledge to assist the student to learn or to create 'software agents' that anticipate their needs and are pro-active on their behalf. Such intelligent agents can, for example, search databases and libraries to assemble and format information which meets an individual's requirements, thereby freeing us to spend more time on productive processes. In medical systems, for example, a combination of all these types of automation is essential to enable the latest information to be sifted and symptoms correlated in order to identify causes, improve diagnostic accuracy, and provide effective treatment. Telepresence systems enable students and experts to 'be there together' and learn, instruct, and guide in a wide variety of at-a-distance situations. These products are exciting, providing encouragement to all ages to enjoy learning. For instance, the CAMNET telepresence product developed at BT Laboratories enables people to learn, create wealth, and help others in ways unimaginable without modern communications. CAMNET has a headset incorporating a microphone, miniature video camera, and display screen.

The person at the far end of the communications link sees precisely what the user of the headset is seeing and can communicate verbally and visually through images and data sent to the user's display screen in the headset. All of these experiences can be augmented by traditional and other learning methods, such as those based on multimedia PC packages. Examples of actual CAMNET applications include:

1. a student and expert communicating about chemical engineering—the student learns while gaining telepresence experience through 'tours' and plant 'visits' around the world;
2. a student of Egyptian archaeology and architecture taking a virtual visit to all the tombs in the Valley of the Kings and an architectural student exploring virtual worlds including new building designs;
3. a student and veterinary expert examining a horse, with the remote vet helping the student diagnose potential problems.

Educational organizations will atrophy and entire national or regional educational sectors will fail if they do not rise to the challenge provided by the powerful array of ICTs available. Other enterprises around the world will seize any opportunity to increase their own customer base. National boundaries will be increasingly bypassed as universities and companies provide education and training direct to customers through global networks. To be successful, economies must create and harness a distributed learning and creativity infrastructure using the technology and know-how available. This is the only way to tap fully the energies and abilities of all the people, each of whom needs to discover ways of learning, creating, and selling new skills which will help them survive in this advanced global economy.

Towards the Creativity Enterprise

People and organizations will need to be ruthless in their decisions about what remnants of the old systems and organizations should be perpetuated into new approaches designed to meet the needs of the emerging experience society. An obsession with keeping and doing old things could become a major cause of 'overload', leading to system breakdown. Universities are particularly vulnerable as they have little financial stock to cushion the mistakes of holding onto a great deal of unnecessary institutional baggage.

Most of these traditional methods were paper-based. This meant many people spent the majority of their time collecting and gathering information before being able to perform any analysis, gain understanding, form a view, take decisions, and act. Most of this work can be eliminated by recording, publishing, and disseminating information electronically and using software agents to do our tedious searching rather than buying, consuming, storing, shifting, collating, filing, searching, stacking, burning, posting paper, and devastating increasing amounts of rain-forest. Instead, books, journals, lecture notes, business briefings, ideas, research results, business games, on-screen experiments, market analyses, animations, video, and other multimedia information can be handled in purely electronic forms.

Young people brought up with digital ICTs often exhibit a great excitement, willingness to learn, and ability to move into the new worlds of electronic information and experience. Older people frequently find all of this bewildering. Making the technology acceptable and friendly to those who are resistant to change, or find it difficult to adapt, is a vital ICT engineering objective. Technology must integrate seamlessly into our lives and surroundings to allow us to feel comfortable in letting go the habits of a lifetime.

An important characteristic of the ICT-based experience society will be the emergence of 'creativity enterprises', such as international virtualized education and training operations. The timescale for which a typical customer may be engaged with such an educational enterprise is likely to be shorter than that traditionally spent in a university, college, or school. The concept of a university having a monopoly over a customer for a period of three or four years will seem increasingly absurd. It will become the norm for people to use the services of a learning company for perhaps one or two hours then move on to another for further sessions at times convenient to them.

In the experience society, we could accumulate thousands of different learning sessions from thousands of different creativity enterprises and individuals. The basic educational notions of 'term-time', standardized 'qualifications', and 'curricula' such as a degree may break-down under such dynamic conditions. The development of round-the-clock creativity enterprises, including entertainment as well as education, spearheads the drive to acquire work- or play-related experience. This is being delivered by the services of an experience industry which is implicitly dependent on ICT for its opening up of international markets and wide-ranging possibilities for co-operative wealth creation.

7

Intelligent Computer-Aided Instruction

Introduction

In recent years there has been increased emphasis on individualized instruction and computer technology specially applying intelligent learning systems that facilitate learning at all levels of education and training.

The intelligent learning systems are known as intelligent tutoring systems (ITS) or intelligent computer-assisted instruction (ICAI). The integral components of any ICAI system may consist of (*a*) the knowledge base: what the learner is to learn, that is, the expert model representing the relevant knowledge in the domain that solves problems like an expert (based on the domain); (*b*) a student model, which may be constructed by comparing the student's performance to the computer-based expert's behaviour on the task; and (*c*) a tutor, that is, a model that should be composed of the desirable properties of a human tutor. The research analytic evidence for ICAI has been reviewed by Littman and Soloway and Wenger.

An example of such an ICAI programme is MicroSEARCH. MicroSEARCH, based on the work of Sleeman, solves deductive-type problems using a heuristic search strategy. The programme allows selection of transformations and examination of the solution tree as the transformations are applied.

Any problem solving requires a certain amount of search. An integral part of AI today is the theory of heuristic search: search that departs from blind trial and error, which makes use of information drawn from the problem domain to guide itself selectively until it finds solutions or goals.

Algorithms in which arbitrary choice is required are known as nondeterministic algorithms. In general, beginning mathematics students react poorly to any use of nondeterministic algorithms. They expect all tasks to be solvable by well defined algorithms. In addition, the teaching system seldom discusses search as a necessary strategy for solving a whole range of tasks. Many tasks in high school and entry-level college mathematics involve nondeterministic searches such as in algebra. Nondeterministic algorithms are currently taught poorly. Students are not taught that search is a legitimate strategy. Sleeman suggested that students should be explicitly asked (*a*) to state all the transformations they consider to be appropriate to the task, and (*b*) to systematically explore the complete solution space. The major disadvantage of this approach is the potential size of the search space.

TSEARCH was built to solve tasks that involved nondeterministic searches. It provided a variety of support facilities for its users. TSEARCH had been implemented using Rutgers LISP on the DEC-10. TSEARCH is a shell for building a class of intelligent tutoring systems. It does not allow the student to type in the transformed expression but merely the number of the transformation to be applied. TSEARCH works only in a domain in which the set of operators are specified. The system presents a problem for the student to solve. The problem is generated by the system or retrieved from a list of problems. The selection procedure of the problem is based on issues specified and the state of the student model. An issue, as stated by Kearsley, is meant to be a method of transforming equations, whether a single transformation or the interaction of several transformations, and represents the skills to be acquired by the student. The transformation is applied to the current expression and results in a new current expression. This generates a tree from the current expressions. The student can backtrack through the tree and pick up other branches. The system automatically redisplays the updated tree after each transformation and analyzes the student's transformation choice. If the choice matches the system's preferred (system domain) choice, then it provides positive feedback. If the student's choice does not match the system's preferred choice, further analysis is required.

Critique of TSEARCH

Sleeman stated that TSEARCH has four shortcomings: (*a*) the major disadvantage of TSEARCH is its speed, (*b*) TSEARCH allows students to be very passive in learning because students can use the HELP facility for a prompt at each stage, (*c*) the task selection algorithm should make use of the information in the transformation matrix to select (appropriate) tasks for the user, and (*d*) the transformation matrix provides valuable information for the type of issue-based coach implemented in the WEST system. Such a coach could occasionally point out better solution paths than those chosen by the user.

The Design of MicroSEARCH

MicroSEARCH is a version of TSEARCH implemented on an IBM PC using Pascal. The following design changes were made between the TSEARCH and MicroSEARCH versions. (*a*) Instead of using all the rules for each type of task, only those known to be relevant are used. (*b*) The system now has two phases: an offline phase that creates the "complete" solution space ("complete" up to some predefined cutoff point), and an online phase that accesses the solution and interacts with the student.

Issues and Concerns Related to MicroSEARCH. Of the issues raised by Sleeman in the last section, the only one addressed to date by MicroSEARCH has been that of speed. As of today application of *Micro*SEARCH is limited to a very specific domain, as in algebra, where only the *simplification section* was programmed and marketed by Park Row. MicroSEARCH encourages students to do a depth-first search of the task space like TSEARCH.

In ICAI the most common instructional strategies have been discovery learning and gaming. Obviously, one discovers error as well as truth. Other approaches such as derived from Component Display Theory have not been implemented. More recently, there have been several systematic attempts to provide instructional information into the design of ICAI systems. Such attempts include the design of a new ICAI tutor and the design of instructional strategies to improve existing ICAI programs. However, neither of these efforts systematically evaluated the resulting "improved" ICAI programs.

We have chosen for the macro strategy O'Neil domain independent instructional strategy to teach problem solving. *Domain* could legitimately refer to subject matter, application area, task, or performance outcome.

Independence can mean "other than" or "as well as" the target domain. *Domain-independent* instructional strategies could mean independent of the subject matter (i.e., strategies independent of math), or independent of the performance outcome (i.e., strategies appropriate both to concept learning and to problem solving), or both. The problem of domain independence, in other words, is a problem of degree of transfer or generalizability. In this chapter, *independence* means independent of subject matter. Thus, domain independent strategies are, in effect, strategies to teach particular performance outcomes, that is, problem solving in the particular domain of algebra.

O'Neil extended this strategy to teach in general a strategy of diagnostic problem solving. They further applied this strategy in the area of electronics, particularly troubleshooting.

We modified and implemented in MicroSEARCH the domain-independent instructional strategies by revising the strategy in Tables given below, and extending their ideas into the teaching of algebra problem solving. Tables 7.4 and 7.5 provide the modifications into algebra.

In summary, the approach in this study was to synthesize and expand instructional strategies described from the following theoretical position: the domainindependent instructional strategies for problem solving provided by O'Neil and component display theory by Merrill.

Component display theory evolved from Merrill and Tennyson's earlier work on designing concept lessons and from their analysis and research to clarify the categories specified by Gagn?. Using component display theory, a given presentation can be segmented into a series of discrete displays.

Table 7.1. Domain-Independent Instructional Strategies (Learning Conditions) to Teach Problem-Solving Outcomes

1. Retrieval of relevant rules and concepts
2. Successive presentation of novel problem situations
3. Demonstration of solutions by student

Component display theory assumes that most cognitive instruction occurs through two modes, *telling or questioning,* and that these modes can be used with two instructional elements, generalities, or examples. In component display theory, learning outcomes are classified in two dimensions: the type of content involved (fact, concept, principle, procedure) and the task level (remember, use, find) required for that content. Nizamuddin provided extensive detail on the instructional design and its implementation in MicroSearch Plus.

Table 7.2. Domain-Independent Instructional Strategy to Teach Diagnostic Problem Solving

1. Define diagnostic problem-solving family to be taught by describing problem-solving characteristics or events pertaining to the family (e.g., "Electrical troubleshooting consists of checking current flow at input and output points.").
2. Communicate a description of the appropriate example device(s) as whole system(s), and the necessary concepts and principles of operation in the order prescribed in Table 7.3.
3. Confirm or teach subordinate skills (e.g., demonstrating how each check is made, how each exchange is done in the example device).
4. Describe and demonstrate appropriate diagnostic problem-solving task strategies to be taught for this application (e.g., select component to test based on malfunction probability).
5. Provide practice using a variety of novel problems requiring the strategies taught, and provide feedback and correction.

Table 7.3. Domain-Independent Instructional Strategy to Teach Diagnostic Problem Solving (Part 2)

Communicate a Description of the Appropriate Example Device(s) as Whole System(s), and the Necessary Concepts and Principles of Operation in the Order Prescribed Here:
1. Present name and brief oerall description of the device including operational controls of inputs and ways in which failures are indicated on the device with examples.
2. Present concepts of causal media in system (e.g., current flow if electrical system, forces if mechanical, etc.).
3. Present concepts of schematic representation and methods of illustrating physical/schematic mapping to be used with exmples
4. Present concept of replaceable units. Present names, locations, and functions of replaceable units using diagrams as needed for examples. Require the student to identify the parts by pointing to them.

5. Teach operation and function (how the system works in terms of inputs, controls, component functions, causal flows, and outputs) of major activating and intermediary components, with reference to schematics and physical layout diagrams, taught by tracing causal paths through components on schematics and referencing physical locations.

Table 7.4. Domain-Independent Instructional Strategy to Teach Algebra Problem Solving as Implemented in MicroSEARCH Plus

1. Define diagnostic problem-solving family to be taught by describing problem-solving characteristics or events pertaining to the family (e.g., "To solve 1st order linear equation," $ax + b = c$).
2. Communicate a description of the appropriate example as a whole problem, and necessary concepts and principles of operation in algebra as shown in Table 7.5.
3. Provide practice, using a variety of novel problems requiring strategies taught, and provide feedback and correction.

The instructional strategies were programmed in Pascal and integrated into the existing MicroSEARCH programme. The ICAI algebra programme MicroSEARCH was developed by Sleeman and was marketed by Park Row Software. This programme reflected the state of the art in cognitive science operating in a personal computer environment. Its predominant instructional strategy was that of a guided discovery approach. The instructional effectiveness of adding our strategies to an existent ICAI shell programme was empirically tested.

An Experimental Study

The altered ICAI programme was compared with the existing package, with three different formats. Students were randomly assigned to each format, that is, the MicroSEARCH test group with only 2 examples and 17 test items, the MicroSEARCH group with 48 problems, and the enhanced instructional design group (MicroSEARCH plus).

It was expected that the experimental group (MicroSEARCH Plus) would perform better than the other groups.

Table 7.5. Domain-Independent Instructional Strategy to Teach Algebra Problem-Solving as Implemented in MicroSEARCH Plus

Communicate a Description of the Appropriate Example as a Whole Problem, and Necessary Concepts and Principles of Operation in Algebra as Shown Here:
1. Present name and brief overall description of the problem including order of operations (e.g., "We are going to solve a Ist order linear equation. For this problem-solving technique you need to separate the variables and constants of the given problem. That is, keep the variables on one side and constants on the other side, by the methods of combining the like terms, etc.").
2. Present concepts and principles of causal information (e.g., equation, solve, addition property of zero, etc.).
3. Present concepts and principles of symbolic representation with examples (e.g., $ax + b = c$, $x = c$, $5x = 10$, $x = 2$, $a + 0 = a$, etc.).
4. Teach procedure (how to solve the problem, e.g., side change, reciprocal, etc.) of major activating and intermediary steps.

Selection of the Sample

The sample was taken from a junior college in Southern California. The students were volunteered from beginning and intermediate algebra classes. We started with 140 subjects. For different reasons such as the student leaving early, computer problems, incomplete data, and so on, 37 students were dropped from the final analysis. A total of 103 valid subjects were entered into a computer that used a programme from the Statistical Package for Social Sciences to analyze the data. This sample (n = 103), with an average age of 25.5 years (SD = 7.79), included 31 males and 72 females. Ethnic distribution as 78 Whites, 7 African-Americans, 8 Latinos, 4 Native Americans, 4 Asians, and 2 other students. To check the homogeneity of the age difference in all three groups a one-way analysis of variance

(ANOVA) was performed. The ANOVA was not statistically significant. Thus the three groups were statistically equivalent on age.

Microsearch

The original MicroSEARCH was developed by Sleeman for one section of elementary algebra, called the *simplification section*. The current state of our MicroSEARCH Plus is for *solving linear equations*, which is another domain of elementary algebra. Linear equations MicroSEARCH Plus has been created in different structures for different groups. The following are the brief descriptions for each group:

1. Two practice problems and 17 test items: The first 2 problems were given for practice. They were similar to the 17 test problems, with no feedback or help. But each subject was assigned a proctor to provide clear understanding of the procedures in MicroSEARCH and the problem itself.

   After finishing the examples, then 17 test items were provided. During the test time, no proctorial help was given. Only two function keys were provided: F3 (NEXT)—leave the current problem and begin the next one; F9 (UNDO)-undo the previous transformation and return the problem to its most recent state.
2. Forty-eight practice problems: This set also was divided into two parts. The first part had 13 problems with advice messages. The second part consisted of 35 problems with no advice messages. Five function keys were available: F1—help; F3 (NEXT)—leave the current problem and begin the next one; F4 (BACK)—Leave the current problem and return to the previous one; F8 (TREE) show solution tree; F9 (UNDO) undo the previous transformation and return the problem to its most recent state, one step backward at a time.

3. Instruction and practice problems: First instruction was provided, then practice problems for each category were provided. The instructional sequence of teaching old and new knowledge of concepts, principles, and procedures to solve an equation using the (*a*) addition, or the (*b*) multiplication property, or (*c*) both addition and multiplication properties is derived from the general model of teaching problem-solving skills. The following modules constitute the instruction:

Module 1. Teach prerequisite *concepts:*

1. Equation.
2. Solve an equation.

Module 2. Teach *prerequisite principle, the addition property of equation:*

1. Teach prerequisite concept, additive inverse.
2. Teach principle, the addition property of equations.

Module 3. Teach *procedure to solve an equation using the addition property of equations:*

1. Teach procedure to solve an equation using the addition property of equations.

Module 4. Teach *prerequisite principle, the multiplication property of equations:*

1. Teach prerequisite concept, reciprocal inverse.
2. Teach principle, the multiplication property of equations.

Module 5. Teach *procedure, to solve an equation using the multiplication property of equations:*

1. Teach prerequisite procedure, remove a coefficient.
2. Teach procedure, to solve an equation using the multiplication property of equations.

Module 6. Teach *procedure, to solve an equation using both the addition and the multiplication properties of equations.*

Module 7. *Integrated practice.*

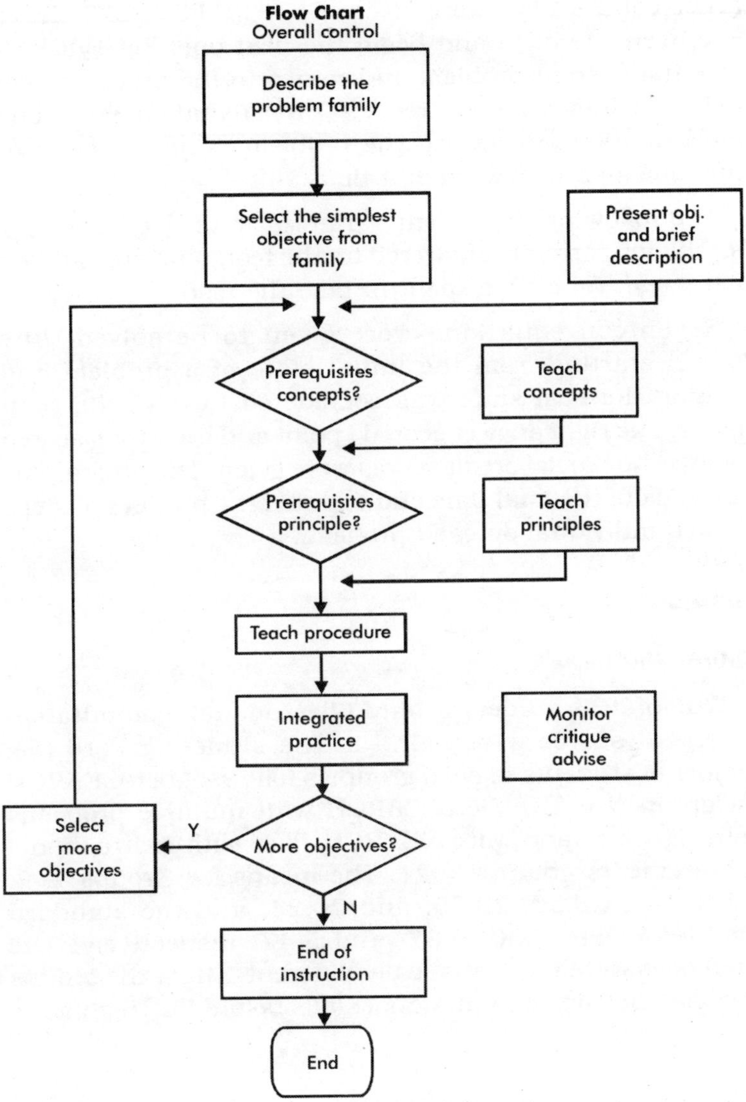

Figure 7.1. Flowchart for domain independent instructional strategy to teach algebra problem-solving as implemented in MicroSEARCH Plus.

Here no advice messages were given. The following learner control keys were given: F1 help; F3 (NEXT) leave the current problem and begin the next one; F4 (BACK)—Leave the current problem and return to the previous one; F8 (TREE) Show solution tree; F9 (UNDO) undo the previous transformation and return the problem to its most recent state, one step backward at a time.

The following dependent variables were used: number of problems correctly answered on the test, total steps taken for the test, total time spent to take the test.

Seventeen equations were given to be solved. Any student starting from the initial state of a problem and reaching the goal state was considered to have the right answer. The right answer scored I point and the wrong scored 0 points. No partial credit scores were given. The programme kept track of the total time and counted the number of steps for each individual on each problem.

Results

Computation Score

Out of 103 students, only 65 students' computation placement scores were found in the student record file; number of students in each group as follows: MicroSEARCH test group N = 22, MicroSEARCH with multiple problems group N = 22, and MicroSEARCH Plus with instructional enhancements group N = 21. The means for Groups 1, 2, and 3 were 20.50, 20.55, and 20.24, and the standard deviations were 7.50, 5.37, and 5.47, respectively. The differences were not statistically different. Thus, the groups were matched on computational skills before the treatments were initiated.

Number of Correct Problems

As may be seen in Table 7.6 on the 17 test questions, the means for MicroSEARCH test group, MicroSEARCH with multiple problems group, and MicroSEARCH Plus with instructional enhancements group were 8.5, 10.2, and 12.3 respectively.

Table 7.6. Performance Measures

Results of Cognitive Test Data (Number of correct test items)	
MicroSEARCH test group	(X=8.5; SD=4.8; n=32)
MicroSEARCH with multiple problem	(X=10.2; SD=4.7; n=36)
MicroSEARCH Plus with instructional enhancements	(X=12.3; SD=3.6; n=35)

It was expected that the instructional design enhanced MicroSEARCH Plus group would exhibit significantly more correct answers than either the MicroSEARCH group with multiple problems and advice messages or the MicroSEARCH test group.

Groups were significantly different; F (2,102) = 6.26, $p < 0.05$. The significant omnibus F-test was followed by the Newman-Keuls post hoc tests. A post hoc Newman-Keuls procedure concluded that the MicroSEARCH test only group and the instructional design enhanced MicroSEARCH Plus group, and the MicroSEARCH group with multiple problems and the instructional design enhanced MicroSEARCH Plus group all were significantly different at the .05 level. MicroSEARCH test only group and MicroSEARCH with multiple practice problems group were not significantly different. That means only advice messages with many problems did not significantly improve the problem-solving skills. On the other hand, instructional design enhanced MicroSEARCH Plus significantly improved problem-solving skills more than the other two groups.

Steps

To complete the 17 test questions the means for MicroSEARCH test group, MicroSEARCH with multiple problems group, and MicroSEARCH Plus group were 203.03,

195.06, and 199.43, and the standard deviations were 131.80, 122,05, and 98.64, respectively.

Time

The mean total times (in min) taken by the students in MicroSEARCH test group, MicroSEARCH with multiple problems group, and MicroSEARCH Plus group to complete the test were 46.10, 25.43, and 28.61, respectively. The standard deviations were 23.96, 11.53, and 19.90, respectively.

It was expected that the instructional design enhanced MicroSEARCH group would take less time than either the MicroSEARCH group with multiple problems and advice messages or a MicroSEARCH test group. Groups were significantly different; $F(2, 102) = 11.45$, $p < .05$. The significant F-test was followed by the Newman-Keuls post hoc tests. Results indicated that MicroSEARCH test only group was different from both MicroSEARCH with multiple problems group and MicroSEARCH Plus with instructional enhancements group. But MicroSEARCH with multiple problems group and MicroSEARCH Plus with instructional enhancements group did not differ significantly, which means both MicroSEARCH with multiple problems and MicroSEARCH Plus with instructional enhancements group took the same amount of time for the test.

It was expected that the instructional design enhanced MicroSEARCH group would generate significantly fewer steps than the MicroSEARCH group with multiple problems and advice messages or a MicroSEARCH test group. However the groups were not significantly different.

The following are important observations from the correlation studies. The total time to complete the test is directly related to the total steps required to finish the test ($r = .61$, $p = .01$). In other words, the total time depends on the number of steps required to finish the test; which is obvious—The more steps, the more time. Similar relationships also were found in total steps in examples and total time in examples ($r = .48$, $p = .01$).

A direct relationship also was discovered in students who took more steps and who consequently got more problems correct ($r = .43$, $p = .01$). Thus, it may be concluded that in a MicroSEARCH-style test, the more steps taken, the better chance there is to get the right answer; one reason may be the goal-oriented state of the system (i.e., variable = constant).

The outcomes of this experiment supported the major research assertion, that students in the enhanced MicroSEARCH Plus group would produce significantly more correct answers than either the MicroSEARCH with multiple problem and advice message or MicroSEARCH test only groups. It was expected that explicit training in problem solving would result in more efficient as well as effective learning.

The findings of this study suggest there is more room for improvements: (*a*) The data from the study could be used formatively to improve the existing enhanced MicroSEARCH Plus programme, and (*b*) a full set of design ideas including other concepts, principles, and procedures that were not implemented, and more emphasis on common errors, could be added. In addition, other facets of component display theory (for example, more extensive use of secondary presentation forms) can be extended.

Conclusion

The design, development, and evaluation of a set of domain independent instructional strategies to teach problem-solving outcomes in algebra through Intelligent Computer-Aided Instruction (ICAI). The ICAI Algebra programme, MicroSEARCH, was developed by Sleeman.

At this time this programme reflected the state of the art of cognitive science in a personal computer environment.

Its predominant instructional strategy was that of a guided discovery approach. Sleeman's approach was augmented by us with two major theoretical positions: the domain-independent instructional strategy for problem solving and component display theory by Merrill. These instructional strategies were programmed in Pascal and integrated into the existing ICAI MicroSEARCH package.

The results indicated that the instructional design enhanced MicroSEARCH Plus with instructional enhancements group exhibited significantly more correct answers on the test than either the MicroSEARCH group with multiple problems or the MicroSEARCH test only group. The results in general supported the rationale that augmenting an ICAI programme with explicit instructional design strategies will lead to improved performance. Shute's (in press) finding on a study of a micro adaptive approach to tutoring, in general, supports the previous rationale.

There are some artificial intelligence-based software packages now on the market. We believe that most of these need some kind of instructional design to be more efficient. To make these packages more useful to the users, we need to combine more ingredients, such as instructional strategies, both at the macro-and micro levels. The state of the art in computer-aided instruction may in this manner be enhanced. The rationale that augmenting an ICAI programme with explicit instructional design strategies will lead to improved performance is supported in this study.

8

IT and Economic Development

Introduction

There has been a growing recognition among economic development specialists that investments in technology can play a critical role in stimulating economic growth and productivity. The rapid economic expansion of Newly Industrializing Economies (NIEs) in East Asia is at least partially attributable to their investment in technologies to upgrade the productivity and competitiveness of export-oriented industries. The economic stagnation of other developing countries has been blamed in part on government policies which restricted the importation of advanced technologies from abroad. IT represents a set of generic technologies with the potential for stimulating substantial economic growth and productivity because they are all-pervasive in their implications for industrial and economic development. Some researchers have therefore made a specific case for the value of investment in IT as a stimulus for economic development and a means of enhancing national competitiveness, including studies that suggest IT development may have led or anticipated economic growth in the East Asian NIEs. Such arguments for IT-led development are based on the notion that investments in IT can accelerate economic growth by enhancing worker productivity and increasing the returns on investment in other capital goods. Our study described in this chapter examined the factors influencing investment in IT and the payoffs they have achieved between 2002 and 2008 in twelve Asia-Pacific countries. These can be classified as:

- Newly Industrializing economies: Hong Kong, Singapore, South Korea, and Taiwan.
- 'Developing' countries: India, Indonesia, Malaysia, Philippines, and Thailand.
- 'Developed' countries: Australia, New Zealand, and Japan.

The study explored the effects of IT investment on the countries' economies to see whether the notion of IT-led development had validity for them. It also examined evidence that would help to shed light on the so-called 'productivity paradox' the notion that investment in IT has not paid off in productivity improvements. We focused our quantitative analysis for this chapter on investment in IT use as measured by investment in computer products and services. A companion study takes a quantitative approach to the factors determining levels of IT production. The IT sector was defined for the study as covering computer hardware, software, and services. Telecommunications, semiconductors, and other electronics industries are treated as part of the IT infrastructure supporting and complementing the production and use of computer products and services.

Investigating the Productivity Paradox

Belief in the ability of an IT-led development policy to spur economic growth runs contrary to empirical research that identified the apparent productivity paradox. That research showed productivity gains in the aggregate economy from the use of IT have been limited, despite the rapid improvement in the price-performance ratio of computers and heavy investment in IT. The identification of the paradox was based largely on the fact that the USA invested heavily in IT during the 1970s and 1980s, yet productivity growth slowed during that period compared to the earlier post-war years.

For example, Roach showed that IT investment in the USA in the service sector from the early 1960s to 2002 grew very tremendously relative to IT investment in manufacturing, with 84 per cent of the nation's multi-billion-dollar IT investment going into services. However, productivity in manufacturing increased during this period, while productivity in the service sector remained stagnant at a level no higher than it was in the mid-1990s.

Other researchers have responded to such 'productivity paradox' findings with disbelief and offered three main explanations for why the expected payoffs might not show up. First, some have argued that errors have arisen because productivity measures based on the level of output for a given level of input fail to account for gains like the availability of new services or improved product quality and variety. Rapid declines in the price of computing power also make it difficult to measure the value of IT stock. In addition, part of the value of IT is that it allows business to be more flexible and do new things, rather than just reducing costs or increasing output.

A second possibility could be that insufficient account has been taken of the way in which new technologies require a learning process and organizational changes before significant benefits are realized. As a result, there is likely to be a lag between the time of investment and the time that benefits show up in productivity gains while organizations learn to exploit IT and make necessary adjustments in management practices and incentives.

These two explanations suggest that we only need better data or a longer timeframe to identify productivity gains from IT investment. The third proposes that IT investments will not increase output: they will only redistribute the pie, benefiting individual firms but not the economy as a whole. This would indicate a global zero-sum game but with the potential for redistribution among nations as some of them benefit from using IT to make their firms more competitive against foreign enterprises. Each of these explanations is plausible, but not very reassuring to business managers or public officials concerned about the return on their large investments in IT. Newer studies attempt to deal with measurement errors and time lags by using larger samples over longer timeframes. Such research has been discovering evidence of significant payoffs from IT investment at the firm level. For example, Brynjolfsson and Hitt of MIT's Sloan School studied data from 380 of the 500 largest US companies from 1987 to 1991, representing over $2 trillion in output (which is about one-third of US GDP). They found a return on investment of 54.2 per cent for computer investments, compared to 4.1 per cent for all other investments. At the national level, previous studies of the economic impacts of IT have been limited primarily to data from some developed Western economies which compared one time period to another. The claims of productivity stagnation were actually based on comparisons with earlier years when productivity gains were greater. Our study pursued the question of returns from IT investment for Asia-Pacific countries at different levels of economic development, measuring relationships between IT investment and output by comparing data across countries over time, rather than relying on comparisons of data on only one country at different time periods.

Environmental Factors Affecting IT Investment

In carrying out the study, we were interested primarily in the answers to two main questions about investment in

IT use: 'What environmental factors affect the level of IT investment in a country?' and 'Does investment in IT lead to increased productivity and economic growth?' We examined these using quantitative analytical techniques to measure the relationship between environmental factors and investment in IT and the effects of IT investment on national productivity and economic growth. We hypothesized that the level and growth of investment in IT at the national level are influenced by four key factors:

1. **National wealth.** This covers the resources to make initial and subsequent technology investments, measured by: GDP level, GDP growth, and savings as a percentage of GDP. Wealthier countries with growing economies and high savings rates should have more capital and more efficient markets to provide investment capital at a lower cost. A lower cost of capital means a higher return on investment.
2. **Wage levels and growth rate.** Wage rates are expected to be correlated with return on IT investment, as organizations paying higher wages stand to gain a higher return from replacing labour or improving labour productivity.
3. **IT infrastructure.** This involves necessary support for the productive application of IT including human resources, capital availability, telecommunications networks, and a dependable power supply. The presence of an adequate infrastructure is expected to be related to the return on investment in IT because the technology is complex and requires supporting networks of electricity, telecommunications, and skilled people.
4. **Price/performance of IT products.** Improvements in the value-for-money gained from IT products make returns on IT investments more attractive because more computing power can be purchased for a given amount of investment. It has been estimated that for every 1 per cent drop in price in

IT products there is a 1.5 per cent increase in demand. The costs and benefits of investment in IT should include relevant taxes, tariffs, and all other factors which affect the price/performance of IT in a given country.

Investment in IT use can improve productivity in two ways. First, IT increases labour productivity directly by substituting for labour or enhancing the productivity of workers. The gains in labour productivity can be seen most easily when computers are installed to perform routine data processing functions and replace workers carrying out those functions. Less visible are the gains in productivity achieved by providing workers with timely information and tools for planning and carrying out their work.

Secondly, IT improves capital productivity by complementing other investments. Plants and equipment can be made more productive through the use of computerized control systems that allow automation of processes and greater flexibility in production. The entire production system can be made more productive through the use of computers for planning and co-ordination of activities within the firm and externally with suppliers and customers. In the service sector, assets can be employed more productively, such as through computerized reservation systems that maximize the usage of airplane capacity. Improved capital productivity should also increase labour productivity, as workers with more productive tools should be more productive themselves.

Payoffs from IT Investments

The analyses in this chapter measure the relationships between environmental factors and IT investment, as well as between IT investment and growth in GDP and productivity. Table 8.1, for example, presents data for each country on key environmental factors affecting IT investment:

1. national wealth is measured by GDP per capita, growth in GDP, and savings rates;
2. IT infrastructure is gauged in terms of human resources (adult literacy, secondary school enrolment, scientists, and engineers), telecommunications, scientific capacity measured as R&D spending, and capital availability (investment as a percentage of GDP);
3. productivity is measured by the level and growth rate of GDP per employee and wage rates by average hourly wages in manufacturing and services.

To compare these data across countries, we use IT investment as a percentage of GDP and of total capital investment in 2000, as well as growth rates for these figures from 2002 to 2008. These provide common measures across countries and over time.

We first looked at the effects of environmental factors on diffusion. To assess the effects of environment, we conducted correlation analyses using measures of the four factors affecting IT investment discussed earlier national wealth, wages, IT infrastructure, and IT price/performance. These were correlated with IT investment as a percentage of GDP and of total capital investment across the countries to find relationships at a given time. Where a statistically significant correlation was found, we concluded that a relationship exists between the two.

Then we carried out correlation analyses of growth rates in IT investment against growth in GDP and labour productivity (GDP per worker) in order to quantify the dynamic relationships among those variables. An especially important aspect was measuring the correlation of growth in IT investment as a percentage of total capital investment against increases in productivity and GDP. These measure the extent to which a shift in capital spending towards IT and away from other investments is related to increases in productivity and GDP, as the proponents of IT-led development suggest it should.

Table 8.1. Key Environmental Variables Related to IT Investment

	Japan	Aust/ NZ	Sing-pore	Hong Kong	South Korea	Taiwan	Malaysia	India	Thai-land	Philip-pines	Indo-nesia
NATIONAL WEALTH											
GDP per capita, 2002 ($US)	22,879	155,283	10,521	10,897	4,968	7,509	2,050	300	1,194	740	520
Average GDP growth, 2002-08	4.62	0.56	6.66	6.68	9.65	8.47	5.81	5.72	8.61	1.18	5.85
Savings as % of GDP, 2008	33	24	41	33	38	23	36	21	26	18	25
INFRASTRUCTURE											
Human Resources Adult literacy (%)	99	99	86	88	95	91	74	43	91	86	74
Secondary school enrolment	96	95	71	69	95	75	53	35	29	66	41
Scientists/Engineers											
per 10,000 pop.	33.8	22.4	23	na	14.9	18	3	12.8	na	1.1	4
Telecommunications											
Telephones per 1,000 pop., 2008	403	435	340	360	209	262	68	4.9	16.8	7	4.3
R&D Capacity											
R&D as % of GDP, 2008	2.8	1.27	0.9	0.6	1.6	0.9	0.3	0.12	0.2		
WAGE RATES (US$)											
Average hourly wage in manufacturing, 2000	11.95	12.43	3.36	2.95	3.95	3.50	0.76	0.50	0.78	0.80	0.40
PRODUCTIVITY (US$)											
Productivity, GDP per employee, 2008	47,301	32,550	19,277	19,895	10,155	14,388	5,694	1,093	2,298	2,067	1,175
Average productivity growth, 2002-08	3.34	0.76	4.70	4.82	6.30	6.02	3.30	4.29	3.84	-0.96	2.23

na = not available

Main Findings from the Quantitative Analyses

Investment in IT Use

Table 8.2 shows for twelve Asia-Pacific countries as of 2008 the total IT spending (hardware, software, services) as a percentage of GDP and of total capital investment. It also specifies their average annual growth rates in spending from 2002 to 2008. In this analysis, we used spending as a percentage of GDP as a comparative measure because it is related to the size of a country's economy.

Table 8.2. IT Investment in Asia-Pacific Countries

	IT investment as % of GDP, 2008	IT investment as as % of total investment, 2008	Average growth in IT investment, 2002-08
Japan	2.18	6.52	13.90
Australia/ New Zealand	2.03	8.24	15.43
Singapore	1.84	3.89	18.06
Hong Kong	1.19	5.18	15.22
South Korea	0.91	2.19	24.49
Taiwan	0.83	3.60	21.64
Malaysia	0.67	2.30	10.77
India	0.37	1.36	22.21
Thailand	0.36	0.83	25.00
Philippines	0.25	2.43	12.21
Indonesia	0.23	0.56	18.09

This is a better measure than IT spending per capita, since it is based on buying power rather than population. (Data for Australia and New Zealand are combined in the original source, so they are treated as one unit using a weighted average of the two countries based on the relative size of their economies.) Two points are clearly illustrated in Table 8.2:

1. Spending is related to national wealth. The developed countries are the heaviest users of IT, followed by the NIEs and then the developing countries.

2. Growth in spending is fastest in the rapidly growing NIEs and Thailand and Indonesia, all of which are playing catch-up with the developed countries.

Environment and Investment

From the data in Table 8.1, we found six variables which have a statistically significant correlation with IT spending:

- *national wealth* measured as GDP per capita;
- *average wages* in manufacturing and services;
- *telecommunications* measured as telephones per 1,000 population;
- *structure of economy* relating to services as a percentage of GDP;
- *human resources* in terms of secondary school enrolment and scientists/engineers per 1,000 population;
- *R&D capacity* as a percentage of GDP.

The first three of these directly overlap with the four main environmental factors determining IT investment hypothesized earlier. In each case, they are strongly correlated with IT investment as a percentage of GDP. Each of the other variables is also strongly correlated with GDP per capita, suggesting that level of wealth may be the key determinant of IT investment. While the other variables might be correlated only with IT spending because of their relationship to wealth, we also found all but two variables (service wages and investment as a percentage of GDP) are correlated with IT investment as a percentage of total investment. This shows that in countries with a favourable environment for IT use, a larger share of total investment goes to IT.

This important fact is not as easily accounted for by the simple argument that richer countries can afford the investment. That does not explain precisely why they choose to invest more heavily in IT as opposed to other investments. A plausible explanation is that these countries can earn a higher return on investment in IT, due to favourable environmental factors. It is also possible that the relationship is the other way around. That is, the reason for the correlation might be that the wealthier countries invested more heavily in IT in the past, so that their current wealth is at least in part a reflection of that investment, rather than the key determinant.

Given the many historical influences which determine relative levels of economic development, it is unlikely that the causality runs in this direction on a static level. Australia, for example, is not likely to be richer than the Philippines because of its higher investment in IT. However, it is possible that there is a dynamic relationship between IT investment and growth in productivity and GDP. This relationship, which is at the heart of the productivity paradox debate, is the focus of the following section.

Table 8.3. Pearson Correlation of Growth in IT Use with Growth in GDP and Productivity

Variable	Average annual growth in IT investment, 2002-08
Average annual GDP growth, 2002-08	0.76
Average annual productivity growth, 2002-08	0.61
*Significance level = 0.05	
**Significance level = 0.01	

Environmental Change and Growth in IT Investment

We now come to the critical question of whether IT investment has measurable effects on productivity and economic growth. We found compelling evidence that both GDP growth and productivity increases are highly correlated with growth in IT investment. More importantly, we discovered that productivity and GDP growth are also correlated with rises in IT as a percentage of total investment. This demonstrates that countries which increase their investment in IT relative to other investments experience higher growth rates in productivity and GDP.

That conclusion challenges the productivity paradox claim that there is no evidence of a relationship between IT investment and productivity growth. It further provides evidence that investment in IT may actually be more productive on average than other non-IT investments. While correlation is not evidence of causality, the findings presented here are consistent with the hypothesis that investment in IT pays off in gains to productivity and economic growth.

The relationship between growth in IT investment as a percentage of total investment and growth in productivity by country. It shows that Thailand, South Korea, India, Taiwan, Indonesia, Singapore, and Hong Kong have experienced the most pronounced shift in investment toward IT, with an average annual growth of over 15 per cent. These countries also have had the highest rates of productivity growth. Australia/ New Zealand and the Philippines are the countries for which productivity growth is low (less than 2 per cent) and appears to lag relative to growth in IT investment. Case studies suggest that the problem in Australia and New Zealand is that both countries depend heavily on exports of agricultural and mineral products. This factor is likely to have overshadowed productivity gains in the manufacturing and service sectors, driving down overall GDP growth. In the Philippines, political upheaval and natural disasters shook the economy for several years.

Challenging the Productivity Paradox

Our study's finding that there is a strong correlation between growth in IT investment and productivity in national economies is consistent with the notion of IT-led development. However, it does not provide conclusive evidence of a causal relationship, given the relatively small proportion of IT in the overall investment picture and the broad array of factors which affect economic growth. It is also true that if there is a causal relationship, the causation may run both ways between economic growth and IT investment.

Nevertheless, this evidence challenges the notion of the productivity paradox. Our quantitative analysis and qualitative case studies of the countries examined lend much support to the view that IT investment, especially in conjunction with investments in the supporting infrastructure, has a positive impact on productivity and economic growth. This is supported by findings of Brynjolfsson and Hitt on the relationship of IT investment to increased productivity in large US companies, which also challenged the 'productivity paradox' by its strong evidence of productivity gains from IT investment. Their information base had the virtue of having a large number of data points, with quite detailed information on both IT investment and company output.

Our findings complement and reinforce those of Brynjolfsson and Hitt. We identified a relationship using data at the national level across a diverse sample of countries. They find a relationship between IT investment and corporate productivity at the company level across a diverse sample of companies within a single country. However, given that the firms in their sample represent one-third of US GDP, they can also be considered representative of the relationship between IT investment and national productivity.

Policy Implications

Our research clearly shows a significant positive correlation over the eight-year period studied between investment in IT and growth in both GDP and productivity. Countries that invested more in IT as a percentage of GDP and of total investment achieved consistently higher growth rates of GDP and productivity. These conclusions have important implications because national governments in many countries have developed, or are developing, policies to promote investment in the production and use of IT, including investment by the government itself.

The development of national industries to produce IT hardware and software has been an important goal of government policies in countries like Singapore, Japan, Korea, Taiwan, and India. Other countries, such as Hong Kong and New Zealand, have taken a hands-off approach, preferring to let the market determine the levels of production and use. The questions facing policy makers are whether there is more value in developing an IT industry or in applying IT to other sectors of the economy-and whether promotion of one will be detrimental to the other.

The benefits of IT use, as well as the high costs of policies which would depress demand for IT, are also clearly demonstrated by the evidence summarized in the chapter. Others have also argued that the use of IT offers greater economic benefits than IT production and that the presence of sophisticated users is vital to developing the production of IT, both to provide a market and because of the importance of close interaction between producers and users. These points of view argue for policies favouring use. If production is to be promoted, it should be done without trade barriers or other policy instruments which protect domestic producers but discourage investment in use by increasing the cost of IT products.

There are still questions as to what the trade-offs are from policies which limit use to encourage production. Japan clearly followed such a policy by limiting access to its domestic market and requiring foreign companies to license their technology to Japanese companies in return for access to the Japanese market. Japan now has a large, technologically advanced computer industry but lags behind the US in IT use. One may reasonably ask what the costs have been to the Japanese economy in terms of lost opportunities to apply IT in other sectors. More importantly, policy makers must consider what the likelihood is of repeating Japan's success in developing a competitive computer industry, given the enormous capital and technology requirements of the industry.

Trends in the 1990s in countries such as Brazil, India, and Mexico have been to remove restrictions on imports, technology transfer, and foreign investment in order to gain access to low-cost IT products and advanced technologies. This trend seems to be an acknowledgement that previous policies to promote production were too costly to user industries in those countries. Countries which have been successful in IT production, such as Singapore, Taiwan, and Korea, have done so largely through attracting multinational computer companies to invest in production facilities or subcontract with local firms. Of these countries, only Korea has used protectionism as a tool for promoting IT production and it did so only for a limited period when it banned imports of microcomputers from 1982 to 1987.

Government officials can be encouraged by the finding that IT investment on a national level is correlated to productivity gains and economic growth. Given the importance of a strong information infrastructure, governments can promote IT investment by investing in human resources and telecommunications networks. This should include broad-based investments such as support for general education and widespread provision of basic telephone services, both of which provide high economic and social returns in their own right.

The development of a good information infrastructure, however, also requires investments in specialized human resources such as electronics engineers, computer scientists, systems analysts, and programmers-as well as specialized telecommunications services, like digital switching, high-speed data transmission, and value-added networks. Such investments may be made in co-operation with the private sector, although experience shows that a government role is usually needed in building infrastructure, especially in NIEs and developing countries.

❒❒❒

9

Impact of Technology on Classroom Instruction

Introduction

It is a description of one of our new measures, a technology-based classroom observation instrument for documenting the impact of technology on classroom instruction. In the report that follows, we explain the need for a new observation tool sensitive to technology impact, and then illustrate the utility of the tool with samples of two of our current approaches to data analysis.

A Technology-Based Classroom Observation Tool

Our ongoing evaluation of the ACOT project required a method for documenting instructional impact and for providing "process" explanations for student and teacher outcomes. The instrument we had in mind would provide fairly comprehensive "snapshots" of classroom activities that would reveal variations in instructional practices related to uses of diverse resources. Based on data produced from informal observations, we needed a tool that could document instruction in different subject areas, determine how particular technology uses limit certain kinds of classroom organizations and support others, describe how teachers' roles may shift when technology is in use, document how the nature of students' work differs when technology resources are in use, and determine whether technology use has an impact on students' responses to instruction (e.g., their engagement with peers, or investment in their work). No existing observation instrument was available to provide us with data appropriate to our needs.

The Limits of Available Observation Instruments for Our Purposes

Many available classroom observation instruments focus on teachers' instructional roles during teacher-student interactions. Two traditions are most prevalent. One approach commonly serves as a "process" partner in process product analyses of functions of classroom talk believed to influence student outcomes; observation schemes derived from this tradition vary in their underlying model of the cognitive functions of interaction in supporting students' learning. A second approach is derived from linguistic or sociolinguistic analyses of discourse. Schemes within this genre are used in investigations of the cultural context of teaching and learning, the functions of language in intellectual activities and the communicative requirements of classroom participation. Across these traditions, observation methods include a considerable range of procedures: on-the-spot coding procedures using either time sampling or event sampling techniques, post observation coding of video- or audiotape, and ethnographic examinations of selected case excerpts.

Although we viewed description of teacher-student interaction as important to our scheme, we considered the available tools inadequate on several counts. First, the varieties of instructional activities represented were incomplete: Within current constructivist interpretations of needed educational reforms, the underlying models of "good teaching" implicit in most classroom interaction instruments are too narrowly focused on the teachers' roles and on classroom talk, and are insufficiently attentive to description of students' activities. Second, the methods for representing instructional resources in these schemes did not reflect the technologies we would be observing. Third, few schemes offered methods of simultaneous coding that would enable us to explore relations among co occurring contexts and events.

Closest in rationale, design, and content to the scheme we envisioned was a coordinated set of instruments developed by Stallings, later adapted by Giesen and Sirotnik and used for two highly regarded large-scale evaluations of school programs: *A Study of Schooling and Follow Through*. The schemes included the Physical Environment Inventory, Daily Summary, Classroom Snapshot, and Five Minute Interaction. These multiple dimensions were helpful guides to our own efforts to design a scheme containing categories that could be cross-classified to produce a broad range of analyses. For example, the Classroom Snapshot captured relations among *activities* (such as demonstration, discussion, work on written assignments), *directors* (teacher, aide, student, group, class, independent), and *group size*. The Five Minute Inventory entailed event recording of classroom interactions: *persons involved, interactions* (e.g., Adult: direct questions, response, imperative, encouragement, monitor/observe; Student: directive, response, refusal, question), *context* (e.g., instruction, behaviour, routines), and *means* (e.g., touching, with humor, with materials, negative affect). We adapted and integrated some of these categories in our own tool.

Because A Study of Schooling data were collected for each scheme at different times of the day, their procedures for observation were not directly useful to our goal for an integrated system. We revised the procedures to enable us to document as much as possible about what was happening at a given time, to permit us to examine relations among co-occurring aspects of classroom activities.

Our Tool

Our goal is to document the characteristics of instruction associated with use of technology resources. If teachers are lecturing, how is the class organized and what resources are in use to support the lecture? When computers are in use, how challenging are students' tasks, how are students working with the teacher and one another, and what proportion of them are engaged in productive interaction? If students are composing long texts or projects, what resources are they using to support their work, and what symbol systems are in use? We developed a versatile, technology-based observation tool that could serve our needs for research and evaluation, and the needs of education professionals for an observation method that can be easily trained and that permits rapid analysis and display of results. In the observation scheme that resulted, instructional activities are the central organizing blocks. The emphasis of the scheme is on capturing the nature of instructional tasks, the roles of teachers, the nature of social relationships, the variety of resources, and the responses of students. The instrument's lbeadth of coverage is coordinated with qualitative techniques for collecting fine grained descriptions of instructional content and process. The instrument uses a time sampling procedure to minimize rater bias, which is likely to be greater if raters sample events (because events are difficult to define when so many instructional characteristics are coded) or if raters make summary judgments over an entire class period. Therefore, with the exception of single-coded indices (the date, teacher observed, and subject area), the observation form is organized for recording in timed intervals. The form is machine scannable, which permits instant updating and rapid analysis of the resulting database. Observers code a set of *activity descriptors* on a time-sampling schedule throughout the period. The activity descriptors are coded once during each 5-min (elementary) or 10-min (secondary) interval. During an observation period, our coders observe for 1 min at the start of each 5- or 10-min interval; they then code just what occurred within that prior minute, and use any remaining time to record field notes. The major categories and codes for the activity descriptors are listed here. Note that, for any given interval, multiple coding is permitted within all categories except classroom organization.

- **Classroom Organization:** Teacher-led, independent work, group/co-operative, group/collaborative (jointly produced product), pair/co-operative, pair/collaborative, pair/tutoring, student-led.
- **Instruction and Support Roles:**
  - *Directing instruction* (codes that apply only to teacher-led classroom organizations): explain/provide information, question (for comprehension or examination), answer students' questions, direct students' work (step by step), correct/grade, test, read to students
  - *Facilitating instruction* (codes that apply to independent, cooperative, and collaborative work): monitor/rove to help students at work, facilitate discussion, conference, joint problem-solve
  - *Management and Discipline: manage, discipline*
  - *Not Present (with the group currently observed)*
- Symbol Systems Serving Key Instructional Functions in the material the teachers make available to students: verbal, numeric, math symbols, graphic, chart, diagram, pictorial, model, map, puzzle/pattern, motor/action, music, objects.
- Instructional Intent expected of students' work: low (emphasis on rote recall), medium (requiring

inference or problem solution within a well-structured problem context), high (requiring inference and construction of a response in a less structured task context).

- Length of the Responses expected of students: repeat/ copy (student replicates provided material exactly e.g., spelling practice, cursive practice, keyboarding drill), select (multiple choice, true/false), short (no more than a sentence in length), medium (no more than a paragraph in length), long (multiparagraph).
- Symbol Systems Students Use in Their Work: verbal, numeric, math symbols, graphic, chart, diagram, pictorial, model, map, puzzle/pattern, motor/ action, music, objects.
- *Resources in Use:*
    - *Textual: textbooks* (textbooks, assigned literature, workbooks/worksheets, tests), print resources (library books, reference books, periodicals, reference/help sheets), materials (paper, file cards, blackboard), student's own work.
    - *Hands on materials*
    - *Computer: instructional software* (electronic worksheet; simulation/ strategy) and applications (word processing, HyperCard, graphics, database, spreadsheet, programming, telecommunications).
    - *Other technology:* laserdisc, scanner, film/video, slide/filmstrip, audio, robotics, class monitor, overhead, MIDI, calculator.
- *Students' Responses to the Activities:*
    - *Appropriateness of students' behavior:* a judgment of the percentage of students who are on task
    - *Students' focus and investment:* a judgment on a 1 to 5 scale.
    - *Productive student-student interaction:* a judgement of the percentage of students who are talking with one another about their work

Results of the time-sampled observations are scanned, analyzed, and displayed in graphic or tabular formats on a Mac II. Currently the resultant displays are catalogued for flexible retrieval using a menu-driven interface; a goal is to develop a user-friendly interface for real-time, online queries.

Illustrative Uses

The instrument provides us with "snapshot" descriptions of classroom instruction that can serve multiple research and development functions. In this chapter we illustrate two of our current uses: documentation of commonly reported changes in high access classrooms, and model-driven descriptions of change.

Documentation of Reported Changes in High Access Classrooms

There is a clear need for empirical documentation of commonly reported changes in classroom practices in high access environments. Researchers and educators have made informal observations that computer use is associated with more challenging projects, less directed teaching and more teacher facilitation, more frequent group projects, more time on task, and more peer assistance. However, there is little empirical documentation of these changes.

Based on observations collected from 1989 through 1991, we have produced preliminary findings bearing on others' informal reports. To preview the findings summarized here: Our analyses to date indicate certain associations between technology use and classroom activities that are consistent with informal reports. But some of our results are not consistent with what now appear to be overly general and overly romantic sketches of technology's impact. Our data suggest that teachers make motivated choices about resources and pedagogical methods based on subject area, and thus their classroom activities are not technology driven in any simple way. Thus our findings serve to underscore the importance of documenting technology impact (*a*) within specific subject areas, (*b*) at particular levels of schooling (e.g., elementary vs. secondary), and (*c*) for specific uses of technology.

We must stress the illustrative nature of our results. Although observations were made of activities that observers and teachers agreed were representative of each teacher's instruction, the data reported here may represent a less than adequate sampling of teachers' instruction: At the elementary level, the database included 145 5-minute intervals (12 hours) in language arts and 73 5-minute intervals (6.1 hours) in mathematics; at the secondary level, the database consisted of 45 10-minute intervals (7.5 hours) in English. The analysis strategy was based on a nested series of queries: We defined a set of resource contexts, beginning with a simple distinction between those where the computer was in use and those where it was not, and compared instructional patterns in those two contexts. We then made further refinements as questions for analysis emerged; for example, how did instruction differ when computers were used for applications (such as word processing) versus instructional courseware? Most analyses of instructional patterns were based on aggregations of individual codes. For example, when we examined instruction and support roles, we created two summary categories: *directing instruction* and *facilitating instruction*, representing the use of any of the roles in those two categories respectively. Inter observer agreement was computed as percent agreement for the aggregated variables we report here. At the elementary level, agreement ranged from 60% to 100%, based on a subset of 83 co-observed 5-minute intervals: Agreement was highest for instructional role variables (82%-93%) and classroom organization (89%-100%), and moderate for instructional intent (70%), length of response (67%), and productive peer interaction (60%).

Reflecting the challenges of multiple coding when intervals are short, the coding disagreements for instructional intent and length of response were most frequently attributed to differences in "what I managed to notice" in each interval (rather than in the appropriate code); therefore our analyses pooled the observations of both raters for each interval. Inter observer agreement at the secondary level was high for all variables (81% to 100%), based on a subset of 27 co-observed 10-minute intervals.

Illustrative Results: Language Arts and Mathematics at One Elementary Site

The results for language arts were more consistent with informal reports of instructional patterns in high access contexts than were the results for mathematics.

- In language arts, computers were in use a bit less than 20% of the time, and uses were always for applications (100% of computer time) rather than for delivery of instructional courseware (0% of computer time). The application in use was a word processor. In mathematics, although computers were observed in use slightly more frequently (32%) than in language arts, there was a striking difference in type of use: Computers were used infrequently for applications (17% of computer time) and always for instructional courseware (100% of computer time).
- In language arts, use of the computer (always for word processing) was associated with independent student work rather than teacher-led work, and with a role for teachers as facilitators of students' work rather than as director and deliverer of information; instruction without computer support was characterized by greater likelihood of teacher-led work and directive teaching. In mathematics, comparisons of instructional characteristics with and without computer support were similar to those for language arts.

- A comparison of mathematics instruction for applications versus instructional courseware revealed that teachers were more likely to be facilitating (rather than directing) students' work only when students were using instructional courseware. Although based on a small number of observation intervals, the pattern does illustrate the importance of examining instructional characteristics in the context of specific uses of technology.

  Reports that technology use supports more challenging student work were supported only by our pilot data for language arts.

- In language arts, tasks were somewhat more challenging and students' responses were somewhat longer when computers were in use (for word processing). In mathematics, tasks were somewhat less challenging and students' responses were somewhat shorter on computer: Students were primarily using instructional courseware for practice of basic skills.)

Table 9.1. Instructional Contexts in Two Elementary Subjects When Computers Were Versus Were Not in Use (Percentage of 5-minute Intervals)

Subject Area	Computers in Use	Computers Not in Use
	Classroom Organizations	
Language arts *(N)*	(23)	(122)
Teacher led	.04	.69
Independent	1.00	.27
Cooperative		.05
Student led		
Mathematics *(N)*	(24)	(49)
Teacher led	.17	.71
Independent	.46	.33
Cooperative	.38	.14
Student led		

	Instructional Roles	
Language arts(N)	*(23)*	*(122)*
Direct		.48
Facilitate	.65	.32
Mathematics *(N)*	*(24)*	*(49)*
Direct	.17	.76
Facilitate	.38	.12

Table 9.2. Instructional Contexts In Elementary Mathematics for Two Uses of Computers (Percentage of 5-minute Intervals When Computers Were in Use)

Observation Category	**Instructional Software**	**Applications**
N	***(24)***	***(24)***
Classroom organizations		
Teacher led	.04	.69
Independent	1.00	.27
Cooperative		.05
Student led		
Instructional roles		
Direct	.17	.50
Facilitate	.38	.50

In summary, instructional patterns observed in these high access classrooms differed both by subject area and by the nature of computer use.

Model-Driven Descriptions of Instructional Change

Our instrument is designed to provide documentation of instructional practices associated with technology use and changes in instructional practices over time. The value of the descriptions we produce is markedly enhanced when descriptions are guided by a model of instructional change: If patterns change over time as predicted by a model, our results provide validation for the model; if patterns are inconsistent with a model of change, our results suggest needed revisions in the model. In this section, our examples illustrate an approach we are taking to model driven methods of data analysis. We have drawn from two frameworks to help us articulate our expectations for instructional impact of high technology access. *Toward a Model of Instructional Change: Two Key Frameworks*. Dwyer, Ringstaff, and Sandholz proposed a model of ACOT teacher change based on analyses of ACOT teachers' regularly dictated audiotape records of their ACOT experience. Dwyer and his colleagues proposed a five-phase process of instructional change:

- Entry: The technology is implemented and a team of teachers is selected.
- Adoption: Basic instructional patterns are maintained, with technology support for drill and practice and for word processing.
- Adaptation: Teachers find that their instructional programme is completed more rapidly and efficiently, freeing time for exploration of new curricula and pedagogy.
- Appropriation: Computer expertise enables experimentation.
- Invention: Teachers invent and implement fundamentally new forms for learning and teaching.

Table 9.3. Task Characteristics in Two Elementary Subjects When Computers Were Versus Were Not in Use (Percentage of 5-minute Intervals)

Subject Area	Computers in Use	Computers Not in Use
	Levels of instructional Intent	
Language arts *(N)*	*(23)*	*(122)*
Low	.04	.33
Medium	.91	.39
High	.09	.03
Mathematics *(N)*	*(24)*	*(49)*
Low	. .42	.12
Medium	.55	.61
High		.02

	Product Item Lengths	
Language arts(N)	*(23)*	*(122)*
Repeat/Copy	.04	.11
Select	.04	.08
Short	.26	.47
Medium	.70	.02
Long	.04	
Mathematics *(N)*	*(24)*	*(49)*
Repeat/Copy		
Select	.25	.26
Short	.71	.55
Medium		.10
Long		

These phases of instructional change can be interpreted as phases in which "technology push" leads to a succession of newly emerging instructional goals. The phase descriptions do not point consistently to particular causes or contexts of change, however. For example, "efficiency" is cited in the transition from adoption to adaptation, but it is not clear how teachers recognize it or choose then to depart from traditional practices. Nor is a particular model of "new forms of learning and teaching" proposed for the Invention Phase.

To provide that model, we adapted ideas from Scardamalia and Bereiter. In their vision of technology-supported instructional environments, technology is a valued resource that can support "learning goals" rather than "task goals." Activities are organized across disciplines, and resources support active construction of understandings via multiple and flexible representations of content. Classroom work requires considerable initiative from the learner over many days if not weeks, and students' products are often lengthy. Learners use a variety of resources, often working cooperatively or collaboratively, and teachers are more often facilitating and supportively guiding students' efforts.

How might our instrument provide descriptions of instruction that could validate or suggest revisions of Dwyer

Table 9.4. Best Fit of the Observation Tool to Dwyer's (1990) Phases of Instructional Change

OBSERVATION CATEGORY	ENTRY (Implementation of Technology Selection of a Team of Teachers)	ADOPTION (Traditional Instruction Instructional Courseware Word Processing)	ADAPTATION (More Rapid Completion of Instruction Time Freed for Exploration)	APPROPRIATION (Experimentation with New Curriculum and Technology Supported Pedagogy)	INVENTION (Learning as Inquiry Knowledge-Building Communities Supported by Technology)
Subject areas	Isolated	Isolated	Isolated Consideration of interdisciplinary possibilities	Experimentation with interdisciplinary work	Integration of subjects interdisciplinary work
Resources	Traditional texts	Traditional texts Instructional courseware Word processing	Traditional texts Instructional course-ware Word processing Local experimentation with other applications and simulations	Declining reliance on texts and instructional courseware Word processing Increasing use of other applications and simulations Experimentation with multimedia Increasing used of print and media resources	Print and media resources Applications software Integrated, interactive multimedia Telecommunications
Task characteristics	Low or Moderate challenge Multiple-choice or short answer responses	Low or moderate challenge	Low or moderate challenge Multiple-choice or short answer responses	Decreasing assigning of basic skills and multiple-choice or short answer tasks	Frequent opportunities for challenging, open-ended, lengthy projects

(Contd.)

OBSERVATION CATEGORY	ENTRY (Implementation of Technology Selection of a Team of Teachers)	ADOPTION (Traditional Instruction Instructional Courseware Word Processing)	ADAPTATION (More Rapid Completion of Instruction Time Freed for Exploration)	APPROPRIATION (Experimentation with New Curriculum and Technology Supported Pedagogy)	INVENTION (Learning as Inquiry Knowledge-Building Communities Supported by Technology)
		Multiple-choice or short answer responses	Written compositions of increasing length	Written compositions of increasing length Experimentation with more challenging and lengthier projects	
Classroom organization	Teacher led Independent	Teacher led Independent	Teacher led less frequent Independent Experimentation with cooperative work	Teacher led less frequent Independent Experimentation with cooperative and collaborative work	Cooperative and collaborative work quite common
Instruction and support roles	Directing Facilitating limited To students' independent work	Directing Facilitating limited to students' independent work	Directing less frequent Facilitating more frequent, and increasingly extended to students' independent writing	Directing less frequent Facilitating more frequent, with experiments in specific techniques such conferencing	Facilitating roles most frequent, and include conferencing and joint problem solving as Use of telecommunications to support interchange with people outside the classroom

et al.'s phases of instructional change? Table 9.4 is an outline of instructional characteristics that can be documented with our instrument and that fit the phases of Dwyer's model, including our Scardamalia- and-Bereiter-like interpretation of Dwyer's "invention" phase. We do recognize that our indices provide only indirect evidence for the phase characteristics. The challenge is to create the best "fit" of the instrument to the model to be investigated, and then to supplement the quantitative observation findings with coordinated qualitative data.

Illustrative Results. Comparisons between language arts instruction at our elementary site and English instruction at our secondary site illustrate how inferences can be made regarding the fit of our observations to various stages. The patterns we found suggested an association between school level and degree of instructional innovation: Compared with the secondary teachers, the elementary level teachers in our samples appeared to be considerably further from the visionary model of inventive, instructional inquiry environments sketched previously.

Subject Area. At the elementary school level, only one core subject-science—was ever double-coded with language arts; field notes indicate that students were engaged in science writing 19% of the time. In contrast, at the secondary site, English was judged as integrated with another subject social studies 66% of the time.

Resources in use. At the elementary level, the resources in use tended to be textual and not technology. Computers were in use 16% of the time. Computers were used exclusively for applications; constructive writing tools word processing—were the applications in use. There were no observations of software providing other forms of representation (e.g., graphics) or multi representational technologies such as laserdisc, video, or audio. Because children were observed to be engaged in drawing and other art and even music activities associated with their language arts curriculum, what we found is that teachers were not yet exploiting the potential of technology to support these same activities.

Table 9.5. Instructional Contexts for English/Language Arts at Two School Levels When Computers Were Versus Were Not in Use (Percentage of Intervals)

Level	Computers in Use	Computers Not in Use
	Classroom Organizations	
Elementary *(N)*	*(23)*	*(122)*
Teacher led	.04	.69
Independent	1.00	.27
Cooperative	--	.05
Student led	--	--
Secondary *(N)*	*(16)*	*(29)*
Teacher led	.06	.86
Independent	.81	--
Cooperative	.62	--
Student led	.12	.13
	Instructional Roles	
Elementary *(N)*	*(23)*	*(122)*
Direct	--	.48
Facilitate	.65	.32
Secondary*(N)*	*(16)*	*(29)*
Direct	.06	.90
Facilitate	.81	--

At the secondary site, the resources in use were also more often textual than technology. Computers were in use here 36% of the time, again exclusively for applications. Here, however, there was some variety in type of applications-word processing (81% of computer time), HyperCard (56% of computer time), and graphics (62% of computer time). In addition, occasional use of interfacing multi representational technologies was noted—audio (6% of computer time) and scanners (69% of computer time). Thus at the secondary site we did observe some technology-based tools for multi representational activities.

Classroom Organization. At the elementary level in language arts, classrooms were generally organized for independent work, and teachers utilized computers heavily as support for independent work. Cooperative work was very rare, and although truly collaborative projects were observed, these activities were not technology supported. At the secondary level in English, classrooms were generally organized for independent work with computer use, and teacher-led instruction off computer. Although cooperative activities were not uncommon on computer, none of these was a collaborative activity.

Instruction and Support Roles. At both the elementary and the secondary levels, teachers were predominantly facilitating instruction when students were on computers, directing instruction when off computer. Students were engaged in productive peer interaction more often with computer support.

Nature of Students' Work. At the elementary level, the language arts tasks were rated predominantly as either medium or low in instructional intent. Thus, teachers tended to assign well-structured activities with teacher-defined criteria for completion. Although teachers were utilizing word processing as support for students' writing, activities in which students participated substantively in planning and coordinating their work were rarely observed. Similarly, students' responses were generally either short or medium in length, and whereas task length tended to be longer with computer support, it was rarely judged as long in any resource context.

In contexts of computer support at the secondary level, although well structured activities with teacher-defined criteria for completion were most common, ill-structured activities (high) were not uncommon. Similarly, students' responses were observed to vary in length, including long. In contexts without computer support, the very low frequency of any recorded observation for instructional intent or response length reflects the finding that students in the secondary classrooms were rarely producing any assigned product without computer support.

Table 9.6. Percentage of Students Engaged in Task-Related Peer Interaction during English/Language Arts at Two School Levels When Computers Were Versus Were Not in Use (Estimates Averaged Over Observed Intervals)

Level	Computers in Use	Computers Not in Use
Elementary *(N)*	*(23)*	*(120)*
Independent work	.43	.36
Cooperative work	--	.63
Secondary *(N)*	*(16)*	*(29)*
Independent work	.52	.20
Cooperative work	.50	--

Table 9.7. Task Characteristics for English/Language Arts at Two School Levels When Computers Were Versus Were Not in Use (Percentage of Observed Intervals)

Level	Computers in Use	Computers Not in Use
	Levels of Instructional Intent	
Elementary *(N)*	*(23)*	*(122)*
Low	.04	.33
Medium	.91	.39
High	.09	.03
Secondary *(N)*	*(16)*	*(29)*
Low	.56	.24
Medium	.69	--
High	.44	--
	Product Item Lengths	
Language arts *(N)*	*(23)*	*(122)*
Repeat/Copy	.04	.11
Select	.04	.08
Short	.26	.47
Medium	.70	.02
Long	.04	--
Mathematics *(N)*	*(16)*	*(29)*
Repeat/Copy	.81	.24
Select	.69	.21
Short	.69	--
Medium	.69	--
Long	.69	--

Interpretation: A Role for Subject Matter Expertise in Teaching. Why might secondary teachers be more able to create opportunities for technology supported, constructive student work? To provide a possible explanation for the results, and therefore a possible explanation for instructional change as described by a model like Dwyer *et al.'s* phase model, we return again to work of Scardamalia and Bereiter.

Scardamalia and Bereiter (in press) argued that students engaged in constructive inquiry must be provided with resources representing multiple kinds of expertise. The kinds of expertise articulated—subject matter, curriculum, and pedagogical—can be distributed among teachers, students themselves, and instructional materials. Thus, although teachers are not seen as solely responsible for providing expertise, as contributors to the design of instructional environments, their expertise certainly helps them to know what is needed to support a given project. Moreover, their own engagement in building personal scholarship subject matter expertise provides a model to students of knowledge-building activities.

Scardamalia and Bereiter did not address directly how kinds of expertise can support constructive uses of technology. It is reasonable to assume, however, based on their arguments, that understandings of a subject's concepts and methods enable teachers to envision how technology might support inquiry within that discipline. If so, then the differences we found in technology use between the elementary- and secondary-level teachers are not surprising given typical differences in subject area training and specialization for teachers at each level. Elementary teachers are curricular and pedagogical generalists within a tradition where curriculum has been defined as a set of discrete facts and concepts not typically based on disciplinary expertise. The secondary teachers are likely to have somewhat greater subject matter knowledge by virtue of the training required of them for certification. Secondary teachers also focus their curriculum development efforts within one subject area. It is likely, then, that subject matter expertise, together with an instructional focus within one subject area, supported ACOT secondary teachers' appropriation of technology's capabilities to support knowledge building and inquiry.

Both sets of teachers, however, have yet to exploit the full potential of technology for fostering deep understanding of subject matter content. There was evidence of some instructional innovation at the secondary level, but the patterns tended to suggest local experimentation (adaptation/appropriation) rather than comprehensive revision (invention). Further work is needed to understand how subject matter expertise, among a range of other factors, plays a role in teachers' construction of new conceptions of instructional environments.

Future Directions

Our larger goal is to develop methods to document the emergent impact of technology on classroom instruction and on student, teacher, and parent outcomes. In this chapter, we described one new tool, our classroom observation instrument, and we demonstrated its value for documenting instruction. We provided two illustrations of its potential uses: documentation of commonly reported observations of instruction in high access classrooms, and validation of models of the role of technology use in instructional change.

The ultimate usefulness of our instrument depends both on its coordination with other kinds of qualitative data gathering and on its validation through planned contrasts, either with classrooms utilizing technology in very different ways or with the ACOT sites themselves over time. Accordingly, we "triangulate" our observations with detailed field notes, teachers' reflections on their instruction in questionnaires and in interviews, and curriculum documentation through analysis of students' and teachers' portfolios. Validity is inferred from comparative analyses of these data sources, from comparisons of ACOT observations collected over time, and from observations of technology from observations of contrasting sites where there are differences in both degree and organization of technology access.

Through its "snapshot" representations of classroom activities, the instrument holds considerable promise as a tool for teachers' professional development as well as for research. ACOT teachers who have piloted the current scannable paper version find it is not difficult to learn to use, and they report that the process of observing with our tool has a positive impact on their understandings of their teaching. The challenge now is to facilitate the rapid translation of teachers' observations into graphs and tables. Using a Macintosh Power book as a platform, Dwyer and his colleagues at Apple are currently adapting the observation tool for teachers' observations of their peers. The outcome will be a tool that helps to bridge the worlds of teachers and researchers, a tool that enhances the likelihood of instructional documentation that can inform improvements in methods of teaching.

❑❑❑

10

Computer Revolution in Education: Future and Scope

Introduction

It is a commonplace that computers and computer-controlled devices offer great promise for revolutionizing education. It is also a commonplace that education is in need of revolutionizing. In the United States, the land of the technological fix, optimists might hope that this situation neatly matches tool and task, with a guaranteed positive outcome. I share the vision, but not the optimism.

Realizing the revolution will require solutions to many knotty problems. There are, of course, a host of technical problems to be overcome in hardware and software design. More challenging, at least to me, are the pedagogical issues raised by the power of computer-based educational technologies: what should be taught, in what order, with what overarching conceptual structures and representations, by what mix of media, in what modes of interaction, and with what roles for student, software, ancillary materials, and teacher? At the root of these pedagogical issues lie even more fundamental questions, questions about how people think, communicate, and learn, questions about the mental processes and data structures we so often take for granted but about which we know so little.

These problems are practical, mundane, and easily overlooked, but they may ultimately prove to be the most difficult ones we face. As a small-scale commercial developer of educational software, I am forced to look at realizing a computer based educational revolution from a business point of view. I find this perspective often sobering, but always instructive. In this view, software development forms only a small part of a much larger system of activities which jointly determine the success or failure of educational computing.

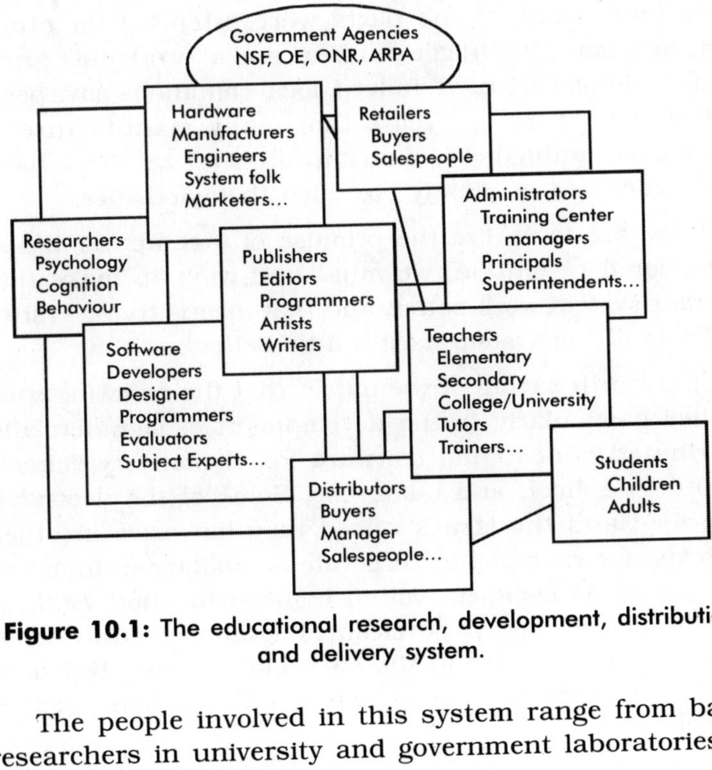

Figure 10.1: The educational research, development, distribution and delivery system.

The people involved in this system range from basic researchers in university and government laboratories at one extreme, to administrators, teachers, parents, and students in a wide variety of educational settings at the other. In between lie a motley collection of hardware manufacturers, software developers, publishers, distributors, and retailers; hovering in the background are various government agencies with missions in education.

Like some giant Rube Goldberg device, all the parts of this complex system must somehow work together to transform advances in computer-based pedagogy into improved learning for students. Outputs must mesh with inputs, and there must be enough energy (recognition, profit, satisfaction) to make all the wheels go 'round'.

Unfortunately, this system tends to wheeze, gasp, and stop rather than hum. As with the original Rube Goldberg inventions, some of the parts were intended for other purposes, many are fragile or balky, and all work only when local conditions are right. Indeed, local conditions have been bad enough in recent years that many manufacturers, developers, publishers, distributors, and retailers have either vanished or greatly curtailed their activities.

If we are to realize the promise of a computer based educational revolution, we must find ways to make this complex system work better, and that means trying first to understand the system itself a little better.

It is worth saying at the outset that the following case applies particularly to the development of commercially distributed educational software for elementary school, secondary school, and home use. Some of the decisions described and the issues raised may not arise in other contexts: for example, in corporate or military training, or in software development within higher education. Still, in the absence of massive governmental support, educational software must survive in the environment described here if it is to reach the many people who could and should benefit from it.

Slide Shop

Currently in the last stages of development, *Slide Shop* is a programme for creating slide shows generated and displayed via computer- "presentation graphics" in the present marketing jargon. People can use the programme to create a set of slides incorporating multi-font text, freehand drawings, selections from libraries of clip art, full screen templates and backgrounds, borders, music, digitized speech, and sound effects. They then create scripts which specify a sequence of slides and slide-change special effects, including cuts, wipes, fades, dissolves, and such exotic transitions as checkerboard wipes and screen smears. The resulting slide shows are stored on auto-run disks created by the programme, from which they can be displayed automatically or manually on the computer, printed on paper, or transferred with narration to videotape.

Issue: Hardware Requirements

No description of educational software is complete without a statement like this:

Slide Shop runs on Apple II™ computers with a minimum of 128K memory, on IBM™ PC, XT, and AT computers and true compatibles equipped with a graphics card and a minimum of 256K memory, and on Tandy™ 1000 series computers with a minimum of 256K memory.

That it should be necessary to make such a statement underlines an important fact: unlike any other successful educational medium, educational software is useless without access to a machine, and a highly specific machine at that.

This stricture has several serious consequences which are often overlooked in the enthusiasm for the latest clever or powerful programme. First, hardware requirements severely limit the size of the available market for educational software. A 1987 survey found just under a million microcomputers in public elementary and secondary schools, including a wide variety of incompatible types as well as outmoded or moribund machines. The same survey in 1986 reported an average of 38 students per microcomputer nationwide, ranging from 14 per machine in Alaska to 135 per machine in Georgia. Whether the aim is aiding a great many students or selling a great many programs, the small number of machines poses a serious barrier. And while this number increased by about 18% between 1986 and 1987, the emphasis in new expenditures is shifting toward software and training rather than hardware.

Second, when administrators, parents, teachers, or students look for solutions to educational problems, hardware requirements place software at a substantial disadvantage compared to other educational media. The most successful media, books and other printed materials, require no hardware at all. And while audiovisual media do require hardware, format standards effectively eliminate restrictions to a single brand or configuration. Therefore, even when a programme has penetrated the market and found its way into a school or home library, it may still be the solution of last resort because hardware logistics-finding the right machine and peripherals in sufficient quantity at the right time and in working order are simply too much for busy people to contemplate.

A third consequence of hardware requirements is the fragmentation of the entire system which creates, distributes, and uses educational software. For each major machine type, there is almost a complete, separate subsystem operating in parallel with all the others. Every action is duplicated several times, with enormous wastage of resources.

Slide Shop, for example, consists of three separate, complete programs, one for the Apple II series, one for MS-DOS computers with CGA graphics, and one for the 16-color graphics of the Tandy 1000 computers. Apple, IBM, and Tandy machines together account for about 80% of the installed base of computers in schools: 56%, 14%, and 9% respectively. Each programme requires different programming, documentation, fonts and clip art, and sample slide shows. Each will be advertised in different magazines and catalogs, distributed through different channels, and sold to people who must be identified in advance as Apple, IBM, or Tandy users.

In short, to have measurable impact (and to survive in a competitive marketplace of products and ideas), educational programs must not only be clever and powerful solutions to educational problems. They must also run on at least two of the most popular microcomputers. They must avoid where possible special hardware requirements (e.g., pointing devices, speech synthesis cards, extended memory or disk space). And they must present the fewest possible barriers to adoption as the solution of choice; in other words, they must be easy to learn and easy to use. Not surprisingly, all this takes work.

Issue: Time, Effort and Money

Slide Shop has required substantial time, effort, and money to produce. Between the first negotiations with the publisher (at which time some of the core programming was already complete) to delivery of the final master disk, more than eighteen months will have elapsed; at least three more will be required before *Slide Shop* appears in catalogs and on shelves. The Apple II programme, exclusive of data areas, occupies about 60 kilobytes, corresponding to about 25,000 lines of 6502 assembly language which required over one person-year to design and write. The IBM and Tandy programs, written in 8086 assembly language under contract, are each about the same size as the Apple programme, and together will require about fifty percent more time to develop. Taken together, the three versions of *Slide Shop* will have required about two and a half person years and a budget of over $100,000 to complete.

Most of the design effort, and at least half of the programming effort, has been directed at making *Slide Shop* easy to learn and easy to use. The programme uses a modified Xerox Star™ or Macintosh™ interface because of that interface's increasing familiarity to users and because its claim to ease of use appears well justified. Using this approach required substantial additional programming and design effort, ranging from programming and organizing pull-down menus to developing disk menus which simplify a novice's access to complex hierarchical file systems.

Further, all of the interface was written from scratch because the corresponding software tools available on more sophisticated machines are not available on the majority of the Apple (nor, of course, MS-DOS) machines now in schools. In addition, very few of the computers in schools are equipped with pointing devices. Those that are so equipped may have joysticks or a graphic pad instead of a mouse. Therefore, to minimize special hardware requirements, the *Slide Shop* interface is written to work with any pointing device and, optionally, with the keyboard alone.

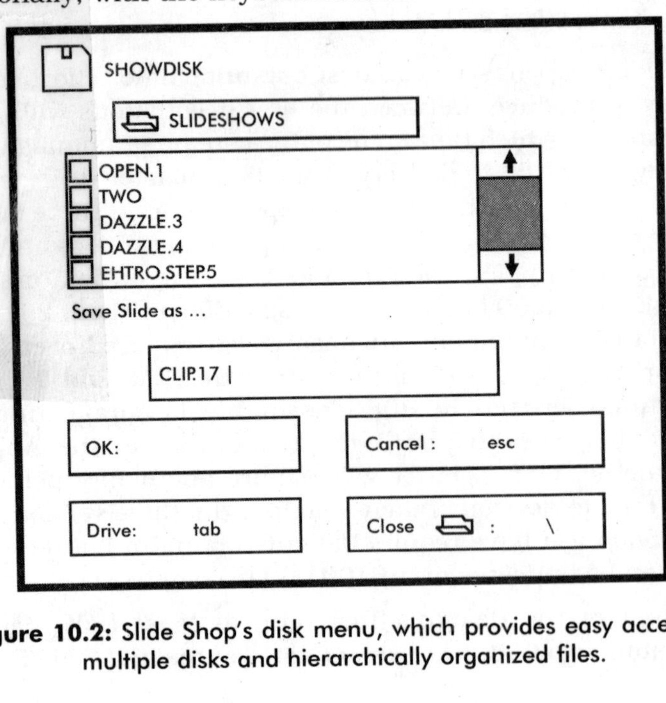

Figure 10.2: Slide Shop's disk menu, which provides easy access to multiple disks and hierarchically organized files.

I believe that *Slide Shop* is representative of the time, effort, and money required to produce commercial-grade educational software; in fact, it may even fall on the low-cost side of the distribution. Using a less sophisticated interface, which has been done in some good educational software, is one way to reduce development costs. Another is to work in high level languages, which speed programming by factors of between two and four, although the same results cannot always be obtained from high level languages as from assembly language. *Slide Shop*, for example, simply could not be written in BASIC, Pascal or C on an Apple IIe or IIc computer.

On the other hand, *Slide Shop* is lacking one important and very costly ingredient of much educational software: *content*. Most subjects reveal new depth and subtlety when freshly viewed by people who are carefully rethinking how they should be taught. And when those people are also seeking ways to incorporate new models of learning and teaching, the effort required including pedagogical design and the necessary formative research as well as interface design and programming—can be very large.

Developing excellent educational software is thus a fiscal as well as a technical and intellectual challenge. In some fortunate circumstances, such as those prevailing in university research departments, the needed support can derive wholly or in part from grants or institutional budgets. Such support is vital for developing high quality, innovative software in difficult subjects. For example, two-thirds of the software identified as exemplary by California's Technology in the Mathematics Curriculum Project received support of this kind. But government and private foundations cannot fund a revolution on their own, and much educational software must be developed on publisher's advances and the expectation of royalties.

IN USA, publisher's contracts frequently forbid discussion of terms (this is the case with *Slide Shop*, for example). Drawing on my own experience and on industry scuttlebutt, however, I can say that advances and royalties have declined rapidly in recent years as publishers discovered how difficult it is to make a profit publishing educational software.

This means, simply, that the average publisher's advance does not cover the average programme development cost. Unless the developer is able to obtain unusually favourable terms (terms in which the advance equals the development cost), the difference must be made up from royalties. In a mix of direct school and retail distribution, the publisher's net proceeds average about 50% of retail price; proceeds from retail-only distribution are typically about 40%.

These gloomy data underscore a simple observation: developing and publishing educational software is not a golden opportunity to advance education and make money simultaneously, as many once thought. It is instead a risky business where pedagogical sophistication and programming ingenuity are no guarantee of success. Sophistication in marketing, alas, becomes a very important ingredient of success.

The Effects of Market Orientation

Slide Shop is educational software in the same sense that a word processor designed for school use is educational software: it provides a tool-rich environment for educational activities such as writing, editing, organizing thoughts and symbols, and so on. *Slide Shop* does not teach history, for example, but teachers and students can each use it to make class presentations in a history course, or to create a videotape show on the American Revolution for younger students.

I chose to write *Slide Shop* in part because I enjoy making tools that enhance people's ability to be creative and to organize their thoughts and mental images into stories, pictures, and presentations. But I also chose *Slide Shop* as a project precisely because its status as a generalized tool gives it the widest possible educational market.

A focus on generalized tools, especially those which cannot be duplicated without a computer, is one important strategy for survival in the uncertain world of educational software. It is not lost on developers and publishers that the best selling school software, notably *Bank Street Writer* and *Print Shop* are such generalized tools. A related approach is evident in the rash of "problem solving" software available. "Problem solving" software normally confronts the student with a simulated environment where logical problems must be solved to succeed. One good example is *The Factory*, where students are challenged to duplicate a target product by arranging processing machines and product orientation steps in a correct sequence. In problem solving software, the emphasis is on generalized skills rather than generalized tools, but the core strategy is the same: maximize the number of people who potentially need and have use for your programme.

There are other strategies as well, of course, all aimed at maximizing the size of the potential market, minimizing development effort and cost or, preferably, both. Capitalizing on the market identified (and sometimes created) by an enormously popular programme is one such strategy. The many printing utilities and shoot-em-up-style drill programs testify to the success of such programs as *Print Shop* and *Math Blaster!*. *Slide Shop*'s name unblushingly alludes to *Print Shop*, because "... *Shop*" now implies a useful programme for creating one's own materials; furthermore, *Slide Shop* allows people to draw on the very large existing libraries of *Print Shop* clip art in creating slides.

Another strategy is to develop software engines, programme frameworks incorporating a standard interface and pedagogical approach which allow the rapid development of an entire series of programs. Although the effort and expense of developing the content of each programme remains, the development of interface and approach can be amortized over the series. This strategy is particularly apparent in software produced by textbook publishers, who are forced by adoption requirements to include software with their texts, but without a significant corresponding increase in total package cost. It is also at the core of such software series as Tom Snyder Production's *Decisions, Decisions*. Not only can a series lower development effort, it can also lower marketing and adoption costs by grouping multiple purchase decisions and teacher training sessions into one. The obverse of this strategy underlies the relative rarity of single subject programs. They are difficult to market and, especially in the case of high quality tutorials, often very expensive to develop.

The most important current strategy is to emphasize software which fits as seamlessly as possible into the everyday life of schools. The reasons are legion, but they all boil down to an attempt to minimize resistance on the part of administrators and teachers who are not already computer enthusiasts. For example, this means developing software that does not require quantities or types of hardware not readily available in schools. It means developing software with interfaces that are recognizable and comfortable to teachers and students. And it also means developing software that teaches what is currently taught, in ways clearly similar to current methods. In short, it means developing software which solves recognized educational problems in understood ways without creating new problems in the process.

Individually, strategies like these may seem reasonable and necessary to ensure the survival of educational software. Together, however, they have a profoundly chilling effect on the potential of educational software to revolutionize education. Not all educational problems are solvable by generalized tools. "Me-too-ism" exacerbates the "hit" mentality of distributors and retailers, limits our vision of what computers can do, and wastes resources on the development of redundant materials. Cost cutting approaches such as series engines tend to shoehorn topics into the simplest frameworks available; they can also promote a centralized approach to educational computing, limiting its potential for more flexible uses. And taking the path of least resistance effectively prevents the kinds of quantum leap we might hope for from a powerful educational technology.

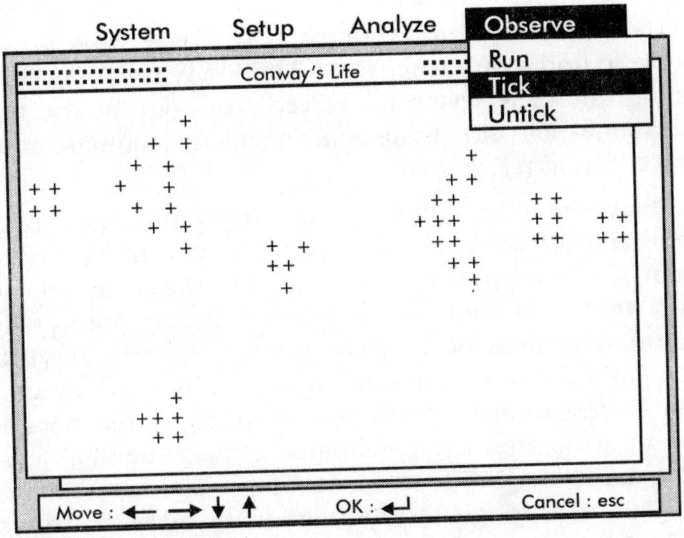

Figure 10.3: A complex system (called the "glider gun") ready for an experimental observation in LifeLab

Summary

LifeLab is a simulated laboratory in which students can observe the behavior of cellular automata, creatures which live in a mathematical grid according to simple life and death rules. Students can create automata with many different rules, and can observe those created by others without having access to the rules. They can conduct experiments designed to discover the unknown rules, create model automata that behave according to their theories, compare the "real" and "theoretical" creatures' behavior, and continue until the theoretical model matches the observed behavior in every detail. The central idea was to create a microworld in which complex behavior was the consequence of simple laws, so that the process of science, the process of discovering laws from carefully contrived experimentation, could be the focus of activity. *LifeLab* uses a keyboard-based Macintosh-like interface, and runs on any Apple II with 64K memory.

The fate of *LifeLab* is instructive: I have thus far been unable to find a publisher for it, and I may never succeed in finding one. The letter I received from one of the major educational software publishers succinctly summarizes why. Here is the letter, *in toto*:

The cases of *LifeLab* and *Slide Shop* represent to me the dilemma that faces us. Computer power does have the potential to revolutionize education, but the system through which that revolution must evolve is hardly optimized for revolutionary activity. In some ways, it is even inimical to it. To get more than gradual change out of this system, we must all researchers, developers, publishers, teachers seek ways to straighten the bent parts, grease the sticky ones, and enlarge the bottlenecks so that major improvements can make it through. A key ingredient, however, must be developing better understanding and communication among the various parts of our system.

❑❑❑

11

Innovation in Telecommunication and IT Regulation

Introduction

The new environment resulting from these developments has raised vital questions about the roles of public policy and market-led initiatives. Among these, the issue of how to balance equity of access for suppliers and customers with the need for improved efficiency in the provision and use of advanced ICT capabilities lies at the heart of many other crucial policies for an information society.

Understanding Technical and Institutional Change

Some people are beguiled by the myth that digital information processing technologies are impelling communication networks towards a future in which competition flourishes to the benefit of all users. However, the problems of transforming technical innovations into commercially viable services are complicated by the fact that there is generally an uneven distribution of the benefits. As markets are imperfect, there is a need for public policy intervention to complement the pressure to increase competition in infrastructure and services. This is necessary to handle the mix of voice, data, and video capabilities, which many refer to as 'telematics', that has been a dominant force since the 1980s. Access to the advanced telematics networks and services of the future may need to be at least as pervasive as access to voice telephony has become in many parts of the world. In order to achieve this, significant innovations in regulation are likely to be required to address emerging disparities in access to common public networks. There are also many unresolved issues concerning the timing and definition of universally accessible advanced networks and services. Questions about who has the power to take decisions with regard to these aspects of the new electronic communication environment are fundamental to the ways in which technical innovations will combine with changes in the regulatory environment. They are essential to the changing balance between:

- Co-operation and competition in the telecommunication industry;
- The economic prospects of suppliers; and
- The way people use and control information in their business and social lives.

Public and private institutions will need to find improved ways of coping with the rapid pace of technological innovation. The relatively slow evolution of communication technologies from signalling using drums and smoke to Alexander Graham Bell's ushering in of the era of telephony in 1876 has been followed by an acceleration in the scope and complexity of new systems that integrate telecommunication and computing technologies. This has involved a move from analogue to digital switching and transmission and from limited computerized control to intelligent software-based functions both within and peripheral to networks. These changes, together with electronic digital media, have radically altered information production, communication, and use.

This has led to an all-pervasive paradigm shift, where widespread benefits are associated with the capacity to apply and integrate advanced telematics services in business organizations and in everyday life. Communication policy responses to the new paradigm have been based generally on the assumption that the development of telematics infrastructure and services would be stimulated by increased competition in the marketplace. One of the early initiatives towards liberalizing telecommunication markets was the creation in 1984 of the Regional Bell Operating Companies (RBOCs) in the US, which broke ATS&T's monopoly as a public telecommunication operator (PTO). Walter Baer demonstrates that certain macro-economic benefits have accrued from the introduction of such competition and case studies in many industry sectors have shown the benefits at the firm level.

The overall quantitative and qualitative evidence may point, on balance, to gains from liberalization. However, this evidence generally documents aggregate economic gains associated with competition and the diffusion of telematics services. These can hide uneven developments in different geographical, social, and economic areas. Public policy and regulatory processes therefore need to monitor disparities more closely in order to address issues regarding disparities in network development and service diffusion patterns. These issues include, for example, the degree to which access to advanced telematics services should approach universality and who should make decisions about how to balance the equity and efficiency considerations.

Regulatory innovations to meet these challenges will emerge from continually negotiated compromises among all actors with a stake in the benefits of an information society. Different national and regional policy traditions, combined with the rapidity of technical change, mean there could be multiple 'correct' answers as to how to organize and manage technical innovation in the communication field.

The Transformation from Telephony to Telematics Services

Comprehensive telematics services from the basic voice telephone connection to very high speed data exchange are the 'nervous system' of an information society. They act as a major determinant of whether regions, countries, firms, and individuals can participate fully in social, cultural, political, and economic life. However, the support needed for more advanced telematics services, such as interactive multimedia applications, often requires performance characteristics that far exceed the capabilities of the public and private networks which reached into the homes of most consumers and businesses in the mid-1990s. The potential users of such innovations range from numerous smaller firms and individual consumers to large multinational business customers, who have much more sophisticated knowledge about all forms of communication services and the applications they need to support them.

Incremental versus Radical Change

Rapid technological change, the unpredictability of consumer demand, and the diversity of innovative applications have created much uncertainty about the speed of development, the diffusion, and the social and economic effects of advanced networks and services. They may evolve incrementally through the gradual interlinking of isolated islands of testbed activity, making access to advanced networks available first to larger businesses, wealthier consumers, and the elite scientific and research communities. Alternatively, a radical upgrading of the public communication infrastructure could precede any clear evidence of strong demand in the marketplace for new applications. The actual rate and timing of the investment needed to achieve ubiquitous access to advanced networks and services will lie along this continuum between incremental and radical change.

Those who favour a predominantly market-led, incremental process of change argue that demand for advanced applications must be clearly demonstrated before steps are taken to create the necessary infrastructure. There are also those who suggest that the early introduction of high-capacity ubiquitous networks would stimulate experimentation and the more rapid take-up of commercially viable advanced services. The assumption is that 'technology push' will create opportunities for innovation and the growth of service markets.

The linking of public policy objectives to a rhetoric which assumes that advanced broadband networks are essential to all forms of social and economic activity was present in the 'information superhighway' debates in the USA and elsewhere in the world. But the vision of an information superhighway itself does little to resolve highly politically charged efficiency and equity debates about how, when, and by whom the necessary investment should be undertaken.

Regulatory Innovations

The combination of rapid technological change and shifts in policy towards creating more competitive market environments has blurred the distinctions between generally available switched networks and dedicated leased network systems, as well as between public and corporate networks. The resulting 'network of networks' is becoming a way of responding to the requirements of businesses of all sizes and to the mass consumer market.

The innovations in regulation and in the structure and organization of governance institutions are taking place at regional as well as national levels in Europe. In the EU, the

European Commission is attempting to shape the overall market environment by introducing directives to stimulate terminal equipment competition, create more transparent procurement rules, and open service and network provision to competition.

Nevertheless, the competitive era in communication has made it increasingly difficult to reach consensus among the many interested parties on a number of key issues such as what the goals of policy should be; the powers and processes of decision making; and the consequences of alternative policy, and regulatory and enforcement mechanisms. It is no longer possible, for example, to advocate simply that traditional public interest or universal service goals should be met.

Questions immediately arise as to what these terms mean and whether they should be abandoned or redefined. For instance, should universal service obligations be placed on network operators to provide services for which there is as yet no proven demand? Variations and changes in these definitions could have critical consequences for consumer lifestyles and the competitiveness of suppliers and business users. These changes will need to be addressed continually.

Historical analyses of the development trajectories of earlier innovations in ICTs will not be sufficient to obtain an understanding of the implications for equity and efficiency in a marketplace characterized by rapid structural and technical innovation. Public policy and associated regulations will also need to be based on analyses that use effective methods of forecasting how these innovations will shape social and economic change and the evolution of networks and services.

Political Economy of Telecommunication

Expectations about the role of technical change in the restructuring of markets need to take account of the degree to which technologies and markets are themselves shaped by the political and industrial environment in which they develop. Change is seldom locked into a technologically determined path. It is therefore useful to examine the political economy of telecommunication and analyse the power relations embedded in processes of technical and institutional change. This perspective offers insights into likely market developments that analyses of behaviour in idealized competitive markets are unable to provide.

Global Strategic Environment

The technical and regulatory changes described earlier have led to such major changes in the global market environment that the domestic arena can no longer be the main focus of national communication policy makers. For instance, Porter argues that the main barrier delaying the arrival of pervasive competition is the time needed for the PTOs of old to learn how to compete in a fully open market where power now resides more with the buyers of telematics services than with the suppliers. However, such claims for the supremacy of 'buyer power' across all segments of the new communication markets are questionable when the magnitude of the equivalent 'supplier power' is considered.

Many larger companies who are major users of communication service are moving towards fully integrated regional structures and are redesigning their core business practices around integrated systems that cross national borders. For example, companies like DuPont, Shell, and Reuters are creating 'logical computing utilities' and building network environments with standardized user interfaces. However, interoperability and other problems continue to make it difficult to obtain services, like billing, on a transparent basis across Europe and to achieve secure network administration and management. Such problems are caused, for example, by the use of proprietary signalling systems, differing leased-circuit prices, and the difficulties of transferring applications between incompatible systems from various computing and telecommunication vendors.

The new order of the telecommunication marketplace is characterized by global oligopolistic rivalry. This is far from a perfectly competitive marketplace in which no individual supplier or buyer can exert undue power. Traditionally, PTOs provided services in foreign markets through bilateral agreements to originate and terminate services and share the resulting revenues. These arrangements have been challenged by a wide range of alliances and ventures that allow operators to enter distant markets directly, including investment in network facilities where liberalization permits. The main players in these initiatives are the small number of major operators who populate global communication markets.

For instance, BT has opened sales offices in the USA to provide end to-end global corporate telematics services and has invested in MCI, the second largest American long-distance telecommunication carrier. AT&T has maintained its historical bilateral relations with BT while opening sales outlets and facilities in the UK and establishing a variety of other facilities across Europe. In Germany, substantial investment in the early 1990s in building up the telecommunication infrastructure in the newly reintegrated eastern states is being followed by investment in Central and East European countries and a search by Deutsche Telekom for alliances with major suppliers in other countries.

At the same time as looking increasingly to international markets for the expansion of their services to serve multinational customers, major PTOs retain considerable 'supplier power' in their domestic markets. For instance, BT dwarfs its competitors in the UK domestic market, which is one of the most liberalized in Europe. In 1995 its network provided some 96 percent of the total exchange line connections in the UK and generated about

85 percent of all local, national, and international call revenues.

Nevertheless, the strength of 'buyer power' in shaping the technical and investment decisions of suppliers is often assumed to be increasing as business customers become more vocal in calling for diversity and change in the communication industry. These customers have become much more visible, for example, as participants in industry standards making activities. Yet there are a wide variety of justifications for such user participation and very little evidence of substantial buyer influence or user consensus on technical standards. Users face substantial difficulties in funding their standards-setting activities and this is not indicative of substantial 'buyer power' in the telematics marketplace.

Co-operation and Competition in the Telecommunication Market

Regulatory institutions can bias strategic management decisions in one direction or another. The main challenge to regulatory innovation in the face of the substantial power of telecommunication suppliers is how to achieve efficiency and equity goals, both of which aim to maximize participation in the electronic communication environments of the future. Significant innovations in regulation are not likely to surface until a serious effort is made to reach consensus on the terms and conditions of network access in a way that gives consideration to both the equity and efficiency concerns of end-users and suppliers. This is not an issue that can be resolved by recourse to straightforward technical modes of regulation.

Seeking to obtain the best possible conditions for the user in terms of quality, choice, and value for money is generally one of the main tasks undertaken by regulators. The most common way of approaching this has been by promoting effective competition and by introducing directives and regulations that are intended to make it impossible for dominant telecommunication operators to prohibit the interconnection of competing networks or to charge unduly high prices for access to their networks. The public statements of incumbent PTOs are like those of any competitor in a marketplace. They all claim to want to compete fairly and to provide world-class telematics services. Nevertheless, the dominant suppliers are fully aware of the market power they can wield. For example, Mannesmann Mobilfunk took two years to agree network access charges with the dominant mobile operator, Deutsche Telekom, despite intervention by the German Government.

Network operators and public policy makers often strike uneasy alliances in the pursuit of their goals. For instance, national public policy generally supports attempts by the traditional monopolistic PTOs to develop positions of strength from which to attack global markets with a high growth potential, such as network management services. Yet public policy initiatives to stimulate competition in domestic markets could merely serve to weaken these PTOs by stimulating intense competition by new entrants who are investing in advanced infrastructure and services.

There are arguments that need to be resolved on both sides of the debate about the degree to which dominant PTOs should be unleashed from domestic restrictions or restrained from engaging in anti-competitive behaviour. This is just one example of the difficult questions arising in the context of the distribution of equity and efficiency gains resulting from market liberalization. The outcome is decisively influenced by regulatory measures affecting pricing, standardization, and—most crucially-network access.

The issue of network access is particularly significant because communication networks and applications like electronic banking have systemic characteristics which make reaching agreements between competing players on a range of technical and procedural agreements a precondition of their diffusion and use. This is similar to the way the integration of railway networks requires a consensus on line gauge, tunnel height, signalling voltage, and other operational factors. Agreements on network interoperability and access for telematics services must, for example, cover costs, transfer payments among operators, and network maintenance. Prices for interconnection and services must not so confuse, or exclude, the customer that the efficiency gains due to competition outweigh equitable access to public networks and new services.

Most suppliers, customers, and regulators also recognize the need for co-operation on issues like national and regional dial-code numbering plans; infrastructure capacity where it is cost-effective; and the technical information required to establish standards and plan the roll-out of new networks. However, they have not reached a consensus on the role of public policy or regulation in ensuring that co-operation actually occurs. Although such co-operation is essential to competition in the new telematics environment, history suggests that firms are not always willing to do so in practice. It is therefore vital that agreement also be reached on the role of public policy or regulation to ensure that co-operation actually occurs.

Regulation may be imperfect, but it will continue to play a crucial role in monitoring, guiding, and sometimes controlling the decisions by major players in the communication market. For example, traditional investment patterns, customer-supplier agreements, and information about networks and customers are especially important to the competitive positions of telematics suppliers. The influence in the market of former monopoly PTOs is strengthened by the advantages conferred by the historical accumulation and control of a strong base of tangible and intangible assets which helps them to protect their market positions. There are very few signs, however, that regulatory innovations are keeping pace with changes in technologies and markets.

Prospects for Innovations in Regulation

In the past, equitable access conditions to the telecommunication network were implicit in the concepts of 'public service' provided under monopoly conditions. Technical innovations have made it possible for network operators to move beyond the control of traditional modes of regulation. This has contributed to an undermining of the consensus on what constitutes the 'public' network or the terms and conditions of access that should be extended to diverse communities of users. If the regulatory process is to keep pace with such changes, it will have to introduce consensus-building measures on actions needed to define and enforce 'universal access' conditions to advanced telematics networks.

Attempts to achieve this consensus have relied on two recognized traditional communication policy and regulation roles. One is to constrain the market power of dominant operators where their activities are anti-competitive or exclusionary; the other is to create incentives for new entrants when market liberalization begins. A third role is necessary to ensure co-ordination in the supply of complex communication systems to prevent equity goals from being jeopardized by the uneven development of the competitive marketplace. This role must seek to provide fair terms of network access to all users by building social and economic objectives into the technical, organizational, and operational conditions that govern market entry.

Liberalization Experiences in the USA and Europe

The USA was the first country to liberalize its telecommunication environment. Its experience has therefore been closely monitored by other countries fearful of 'falling behind'. In considering possible options the significant differences, as well as similarities, between US and European regulatory experiences and environments should be taken into account.

The first signs of competitive entry in the US market were felt in the 1950s, when a small device called the Hush-a-Phone allowed a caller to shield sound from nearby listeners. Full terminal equipment competition took two more decades to establish. In public network service supply, AT&T was challenged in the late 1950s by private telecommunication users who won access to the radio spectrum to provide microwave services. Discount pricing strategies, proprietary standards, and reluctance to interconnect competing networks were the tools used by AT&T to rebuff challenges to its market.

By the 1990s there was a growing tendency in the USA to rely on regulation of technical standards with, for example, the dominant carriers having to submit network architecture plans to the regulatory agency, the Federal Communications Commission (FCC). This followed numerous inquiries, the break-up of AT&T, and the introduction of Open Network Architecture (ONA) arrangements which require the Bell Regional Operating Companies to unbundle their services, with competitors having access to their networks.

Such technical approaches to regulation have not succeeded in prising open public networks, at least not in the way many customers and competitors would like. Services have not been sufficiently unbundled to eliminate barriers to new entry, especially in local or regional markets. Rivalry in the marketplace has still favoured the larger telecommunication users in terms of choice and the costs of services. And US regulatory institutions are continuing to have difficulty coping with technical change.

In the EU, market liberalization came later and moved comparatively more rapidly in some member states, like the UK, and regions, such as Northern versus Southern Europe. Nevertheless, there are similarities, such as the way competition has created an increasing need for co-operation and imaginative regulatory innovation. There are glimpses of such innovation in the British Government's policy of promoting local network competition in advance of the US market. But there are few signs of innovation in the way regulators are attempting to control the market power of dominant PTOs. For example, the 'level playing-field' is being sought in the UK mainly through the use of technical standards and price regulations, which is an approach similar to that adopted in the USA.

However, the USA may not provide a good model of regulatory innovation for Europe. The USA has produced detailed procedures of administrative oversight and cost-accounting methods for assessing whether service prices are fair. In turn, this system has built a vast edifice of information requirements and an immense bureaucracy of legal experts, economists, and public interest advocates. European policy makers appear to be moving down a very similar path in grappling with the increasing plurality of networks, motivated by the belief that regulation of this kind can help to avoid what Baer calls the 'costs of delay' in introducing competition. This runs the risk of recreating the features of American public utility regulation which have been found wanting.

In both the USA and Europe, public policy-making institutions have found it difficult to promote debate on how, and for whom, the public telematics infrastructure should be designed. Public networks generally are being designed to meet the stringent requirements of large customers, which outstrip the average quality and capabilities of the public network and have a high implementation cost. Historical discrepancies are likely to continue between the technical standards and pricing structures needed to meet the requirements of the majority of smaller customers and those required to support advanced services for transnational corporations.

The dominant PTOs have an incentive to invest heavily to meet the needs of the multinational firms who generate a significant proportion of their revenues. This is not a conspiracy or the result of collusion among these operators. It is a pragmatic response to the internationalization of markets. The outcome of rivalry among the major operators will obviously make a difference to consumers, but the technical and public policy design principles under which the winners operate are even more important. These principles will affect whether a network is open or closed in respect of who may have access to it; who determines the network's specific uses; who may supply content; who can provide the equipment used; how interfaces and standards are formulated; and whether the technical details are made public or kept private.

Need for Radical Regulatory Innovation

Technical modes of regulation cannot on their own resolve such issues in a way that gives adequate consideration both to equity and efficiency concerns. A serious effort to reach consensus on the public service goals to be met in a competitive market environment must be based on significant innovations in regulations that take account of the political and economic environment in which new technologies are applied.

One practical step which could help to achieve this would be to require incumbent network operators to separate structurally the provision of a public access network from their other global and domestic operations. This would unleash these companies to confront the full force of oligopolistic rivalry in international markets, perhaps causing some PTOs to withdraw from certain parts of the domestic infrastructure. All network operators licensed to provide access to end-user customers would then face the same set of incentives to negotiate interconnection arrangements to complete the systemic features of their networks, which involves being able both to originate and terminate services. Their choices concerning service portfolios, network configurations, and the ubiquity of network access would become more transparently a function of the costs of network access and of market characteristics. This contrasts with the opaque result of the impact of the market power of dominant vertically integrated PTOs.

An alternative to structural separation would be the use of accounting mechanisms which are being explored in the EU. However, as the US experience has illustrated, the accompanying bureaucracy which proliferates under this approach and the extent to which methodologies are subject to dispute suggests that this is by far a second-best option.

Either of these steps would represent an incremental innovation, but this would not be a sufficient response to the transformations in telematics service markets. There is also a necessary corollary measure. As liberalization and competition take hold, the larger operators will pursue their goals in international markets and new entrants will begin to provide alternative network access services—but the quality and characteristics of services will be uneven. This means there will continue to be a need to ensure that a common public network evolves. Failure to address this issue is likely to result in the exclusion of certain users from what many regard as essential access to the 'information highways' of the future. This could arise from the larger operators' pursuit of business goals in international markets and the uneven diffusion of alternative network access services provided by new entrants.

The problem is not one of specifying which network configurations, features, or services must be accessible to various communities of users. It is one of creating the institutional environment in which such issues can be meaningfully debated on an ongoing basis as technologies change and markets are restructured. Radical regulatory innovation is necessary to build such an environment. Too often the process of consensus formation becomes stalled in highly charged debates about interpretations of the 'relevant' costs of service supply, the impact of pricing strategies, and the details of technical standards. Conflicting views of the appropriate unfolding of a balance between equity and efficiency considerations are deeply embedded in these debates.

Achieving Consensus on Equity and Efficiency

One major goal of radical regulatory innovation is to institutionalize a means of establishing a consensus over time on the minimum set of telematics services needed to meet public service requirements. At one extreme, for example, it might be decided that simple access to a copper wire pair at a reasonable price is all that is needed. At the other, access to fibre-based networks and very high speed information applications could be required on a universal basis. In between lies the reality of network and service investment decisions guided by the pressures of a global marketplace and economic efficiency considerations.

Radical regulatory innovation would redirect activity to a minimum set of essential and manageable tasks, such as promoting the development of telematics networks designed to optimize access for the majority of users. Dominant PTOs in liberalized markets are likely to agree with such an approach as an alternative to regulation which seeks to manage or replicate the decisions of network operators through the detailed scrutiny of their commercial strategic decisions. Other regulatory priorities include:

1. monitoring where gaps are appearing geographically and demographically as a result of uneven market development;
2. investigating the degree to which public access to telematics networks and services is technically or economically feasible;
3. encouraging effective and ongoing supplier and user participation in decision making forums with a clear remit to recommend intervention to redress imbalances in network access.

Any such policies will be politically controversial as they have far reaching economic consequences, including consideration of when, how, and to what extent public financing is needed to strengthen incentives for investment in infrastructure and services. Nevertheless, public intervention in the name of public service and equity considerations is not only possible; it is essential. To paraphrase Mumford, the problem of integrating the machine in society is not merely a matter of making social institutions keep in step with the machine. The problem is also one of altering the nature and rhythm of machines to fit the actual needs of the community. A machine, like a telematics network, is a good example of where it is necessary to ensure that network design and implementation reflect the broadest possible range of user requirements.

Network Interconnection: A Focus for the Future

The strong forces of global competition often appear to be moving regulation of communication markets beyond the control of individual countries. However, communication traffic originates and terminates within national boundaries. It will therefore remain feasible to establish a policy and regulatory apparatus to shape the design of national or regional markets in the interests of a wide range of social and economic goals. These include the desirability of dislodging the traditional monopoly players as well as ensuring that competition does not erode resources for innovation and for social and economic experimentation with new advanced applications. The link between such issues is being recognized at the level of general policy, for example, in discussions on the information-'poor' and the information-'rich'. Nevertheless, there is a lack of consensus on how to bring about policy and regulatory innovations in practice.

There is a vital need for policy and regulatory institutions to cooperate closely in jointly addressing innovation, competition, and social objectives. Network interconnection issues are central to the ways communication markets evolve. They provide a focus for creative institution building on a regional basis. Interconnection policies and practices can be used to promote incentives for investment; the wider geographical distribution, accessibility, and affordability of services; and the provision of specialized and other services to meet social and regional requirements.

Policy and regulatory developments along these lines will be effective only if they are given the highest political priority. Regional institution building brings fears of the rise of a labyrinthine centralized regulatory apparatus. These fears can be countered by showing that a concentration on resolving interconnection issues can reduce the need for traditional forms of policy and regulation which are increasingly ineffective in markets populated by many suppliers. Any benefits gained by some suppliers and users from a failure to engage policy and regulatory resources in this way are likely to be short-lived. Focusing on interconnection will be a sign of radical innovation in the regulatory process, rather than the withering away of regulation.

Ricardo suggested that 'where there is free competition, the interests of the individual and that of the community are *never* at variance'. However, there is evidence that 'information highway' markets are not truly free, because of the history of public policy measures in many countries and the need to co-ordinate complex networks. While there is increasing choice and diversity and a downward pressure on some prices in telematics services markets, the need to recover co-ordination costs and the monopolization strategies of certain suppliers also lead to cost increases. Public policies are needed to build a consensus on the need for, and the means to achieve, 'universal' telematics services. This would avert a tragedy in the form of the demise of an accessible and affordable public network.

❑❑❑

Index

A

Advanced Research Projects Agency (ARPA), 129
Advertise Control Options, 96
Analysis of Variance, 182
Analytical Engine, 103

B

Bank Street Writer, 239
BBC Micro, 12
Blank Space, 72
Bluetooth, 132
Border Gateway Protocol, 138
Boston's Artificial Intelligence Laboratory, 15
Bulletin Board System, 13
Bus Network Topology, 145

C

Campus Network, 135
Central Processing Unit, 54
Classroom Organization, 223
Coaxial Cable, 131
Communication Problems, 70
Compuserve Information Service (CIS), 13
Computer Curriculum
Corporation (CCC), 44
Network, 129
Assisted Learning, 32
Based Pedagogy, 231
Computers: Social Revolution in Education, 102
Connection Method, 130
Copyright Issues, 64

D

Daisy Chains, 152
Design Challenges, 69
of Microsearch, 177
Desktop Publishing Programs, 25
Digital Subscriber Line, 135
Directing Instruction, 214
Disk Operating System, 55
Distributed Bus, 146

E

Education Monopolies, 162
Educational Software, 52
Enterprise Private Network, 136
Extended Star, 148

F

Facilitating Instruction, 211
Federal Communications Commission (FCC), 255
Floppy Disk, 54
Freeware, 63

G

Global Area Network, 136
Strategic Environment, 249
Graphical User Interface, 31

H

Highlight Sparingly, 76
Home Area Network, 135
Style Learning, 21
Hyperspace, 167
Hyperstudio, 57

I

ICT-Based Revolution, 157
Ignore Blank Inputs, 89
Incremental Display-Building, 77
Industrial Revolution, 167
Information Superhighway, 247
Inner London Educational Computing Centre, 33
Integrated Digital Services Network (ISDN) Service, 170
Learning Systems, 43
Integrating the Learning Structure, 161
Intelligent Computer-Aided Instruction, 175
Tutoring Systems, 175
Interactive Theatre, 171
Internet, 137
Relay Chat, 13
Internetwork, 137

L

Learning Goals, 219
Lifelab, 241
Linear Bus, 145
Local Area Network, 134
Logical Computing Utilities, 249
Topology, 151

M

Macintosh Operating System, 55
Macrohybridization, 161
Massachusetts Institute of Technology (MIT), 14
Mathematics Curriculum Project, 237
Maths with A Story, 34
Micro-Hybridization, 160
Microprocessor, 54
Microsearch, 183
Mix Text and Pictures, 74
Model-Driven Descriptions of Instructional Change, 217
Multimedia Enhances Education, 166
Multistation Access Unit, 156

N

National Environmental Database (NED), 36
Nervous System, 246
Network Interface Cards, 140
Nonbroadcast Multi-Access (NBMA), 148

O

On-Screen Instructions, 87
Operating System, 54
Optical Fiber Cable, 131
Overlay Network, 139

P

Personal Area Network, 133
Perspectives Interactives Paradigm, 40
Physical Environment Inventory, 209

Topologies, 144
Political Economy of Telecommunication, 248
Presentation Graphics, 232
Print Shop, 239
Problem Solving, 239
Productive Student-Student Interaction, 212
Public Telecommunication Operator (PTO), 245

R

Rapid Technological Change, 246
Read-Only Memory (ROM), 54
Regional Bell Operating Companies (RBOCs), 245
Regulatory Innovations, 247
Resilient Overlay Network, 140
Revolutionizing Education, 164
Ring Network Topology, 148
Robot Software, 13
ROM, 54
Routers, 142

S

School-Style Learning, 21
Service Level Agreement (SLA), 137
Shareware, 64
Signal Topology, 151
Site License, 65
Slide Shop, 232
Social Revolution in Education, 102
Solving Linear Equations, 183
Spell Checker, 126
Star Bus Network, 156
Network Topology, 146
Ring Network, 156
Subject Area, 222
Supplier Power, 250
Switches, 142

T

Task Goals, 219
Technology Push, 219
Zealots, 29
Based Classroom Observation Tool, 207
Telecommunications and Competition, 159
Telematics, 244
Teleported, 169
Terrestrial Microwave, 131
Text IS Graphics, 73
The Ada Project (TAP), 104
Connected Family, 22
Transforming Education, 160
Tree Network Topology, 150
TSEARCH, 177
Twisted Pair Wire, 130

U

User Control, 93
User-Interface Design, 13

V

Verbal Input, 89
Virtual Private Network, 137
Universities, 170
Virtualizing Education, 163
Visual Medium, 70

W

Wide Area Network, 135
Windows, 55
Wired Technologies, 130
Wireless Technologies, 131

❑❑❑

30. A Text Book of Environmental Studies 175/-
31. Teaching of History 175/-
32. Administrative Thinkers 175/-
33. Research Methodology 175/-
34. Curriculum Development 195/-
35. Teaching of Science 160/-
36. Teaching of Mathematics 160/-
37. Principles of Educational &Vocational Guidance 175/-
38. Child Psychology 175/-
39. Abnormal Psychology 175/-
40. Indian Education in Emerging Society 175/-
41. Human Resource Management 160/-
42. Higher Education and Global Challenges 175/-
43. Teaching of Geography 150/-
44. Teaching of Social Studies 150/-
45. Teaching of English 175/-
46. Principles of Office Management **(Revised Ed.)** 250/-
47. Education for All: The Indian Saga 175/-
48. Value Education in Global Perspective 175/-
49. Teacher Training 150/-
50. Public Administration 150/-
51. Public Relations & Integrated Communications 195/-
52. Educational Psychology 150/-
53. Introduction to Educational Technology 175/-
54. Textbook of Food and Nutrition 150/-

Lotus PRESS

4263/3, Ansari Road,
Darya Ganj, New Delhi-110 002
Ph.: 32903912, 23280047,9811594448
E-mail: lotus_press@sify.com
www.lotuspress.co.in